Microsoft Office Live Small Business
Beginner's Guide

Build and customize your small business website

Rahul Pitre

PUBLISHING

BIRMINGHAM - MUMBAI

Microsoft Office Live Small Business

First published: November 2009

Production Reference: 1191109

Published by Packt Publishing Ltd.
32 Lincoln Road
Olton
Birmingham, B27 6PA, UK.

ISBN 978-1-847198-74-7

www.packtpub.com

Cover Image by Parag Kadam (paragvkadam@gmail.com)

Credits

Author

Rahul Pitre

Reviewers

Maarten van Stam

Vivek Thangaswamy

David M.Wenning

Acquisition Editor

James Lumsden

Development Editor

Amey Kanse

Technical Editor

Tarun Singh

Copy Editor

Ajay Shanker

Indexer

Hemangini Bari

Editorial Team Leader

Abhijeet Deobhakta

Project Team Leader

Priya Mukherjee

Project Coordinator

Leena Purkait

Proofreader

Andie Scothern

Graphics

Nilesh Mohite

Production Coordinator

Aparna Bhagat

Cover Work

Aparna Bhagat

About the Author

Rahul Pitre has been writing software of one sort or another for 25 years, the last dozen or so of which he has spent mostly developing websites and web applications. He runs Acxede, a software consulting and training firm in New York, where he oversees web application and content development for a variety of clients. He holds masters degrees in Business Administration and Computer Information Systems.

Acknowledgments

Several people contributed significantly to this book in one way or another, and I'd like to express my sincere gratitude to them.

Thanks to James Lumsden, Acquisition Editor at Packt Publishing, for making this book possible. Thanks to Amey Kanse, Development Editor, for guiding me throughout its writing; his advice was invaluable. Thanks to Leena Purkait, Project Coordinator, for keeping the book on schedule; she managed to do so despite my occasional bouts of inertia.

Thanks to Abhijeet Deobhakta, Editorial Team Leader, and to Priya Mukherjee, Project Team Leader, for overseeing the creation of this book.

Thanks to Tarun Singh, Technical Editor, for accommodating several last-minute changes to the manuscript without losing his cool. Thanks to Ajay Shankar, Copy Editor, for performing the unenviable task of correcting my grammar and to Andie Scothern for ably proofreading the final manuscript. Thanks go to Hemangini Bari for indexing the book. Thanks also go to Aparna Bhagat for designing the pretty cover as well as for the neat layout of the book.

Thanks go to Dave Wenning, Maarten van Stam, and Vivek Thangaswamy for painstakingly reviewing the manuscript; they caught my mistakes and made countless suggestions. Their hard work has kept me honest and helped me write a better book.

Finally, thanks go to three people who probably will never read this book. Thanks to my son Rohan and my daughter Ruhi for promising to buy it nevertheless. And thanks to my wife Minal for putting up with me and managing our family in spite of me while I wrote this book.

All these folks deserve as much credit for this book as I do.

About the Reviewers

Maarten van Stam holds a B.Sc in Computer science (graduation in 1996, HIO, The Hague, The Netherlands) and worked as a software engineer for over 20 years. He started programming dBase and Clipper (DOS) systems in the early 80s, followed by Pascal and C++ in the late 80s, C++/VB "for Windows" in the early 90s, and continues to program in VB.NET and C# as part of the Microsoft's .NET Framework.

Maarten has specialized in Office development, .NET, and VSTO and has received the Microsoft MVP award in the expertise area of Visual Developer—VSTO for voluntarily sharing expertise with others. In addition to this role, Maarten takes part in several TAP Programs, beta tests, software design reviews, and advisory councils for software tools such as Visual Studio Team System and Microsoft Office. In addition to working in the software business professionally, Maarten is also an organizational member of the Software Development Network, currently the largest developer community group in the Netherlands (www.sdn.nl).

Besides tech reading this book, Maarten also reviewed *Visual Studio Tools for Office 2007: VSTO for Excel, Word, and Outlook* by Packt Publishing, authored by Eric Carter and Eric Lippert, Maarten's insights can be read and followed on www.maartenvanstam.nl, where you can find his blog that relates to all aspects of software development.

Vivek Thangaswamy is a software solutions developer and technical author living and working in the pleasant surroundings of Chennai, India. His range of technical competence stretches across platforms and lines of business, but he specializes in Microsoft Enterprise application architectures and Microsoft Server-based product integrations. Vivek is currently working for the world's largest software services company in Microsoft Technologies. He holds several Microsoft certifications and Microsoft MVP awards. He has a wide range of technology experience. Vivek started programming in a DOS world, then moved to C, C++, VC++, VB 6, ASP 3.0; and eventually to .NET in both VB.NET and C# worlds and also in ASP.NET/MS SQL Server 2005. He has a very good experience in Enterprise Collaboration Microsoft Office SharePoint Server 2007 accompanied with the VSTO and .NET 3.0 frameworks. He started working in SharePoint from version 2003. Currently working with Windows Workflow Foundations and Windows Communication Foundations, he has very good exposure to Microsoft Commerce Server and Performance Point Server. Apart from Microsoft Technologies, Vivek has an expertise in PHP, ColdFusion, MySQL, and PostgreSQL. He has UI design skills using Photoshop and Flash, and has major interest in exploring open source technologies and innovating through them. He has completed his Bachelor of Technology degree in Information Technology from one of the world's finest universities and is currently pursuing the Management of Business Administration in Finance degree.

Vivek has also authored the book *VSTO 3.0 for Office 2007 Programming* by Packt Publishing (`http://www.packtpub.com/vsto-3-for-office-2007-programming/book`), which released in March 2009.

David M. Wenning is a hospital pharmacist. His interest in computer technology dates back to graduate school in the 1970s. He became interested in applying computer technology to pharmacy practice, and took elective courses in programming languages and business computing. In the early 1980s, the IBM PC was released and he purchased one of the first ones available. The computer became an indispensable tool in both, his professional and personal lives.

Next came the Internet. Already a weather hobbyist, he had a yen to publish his weather station data to the Web. He became aware of the Microsoft Office Live Small Business platform and took them up on their offer for a free website under their beta testing program. It quite turned out to be the right choice for him. He had a good understanding of computer technology, but no familiarity with web design or construction. Office Live made the process easy and he has been using the service for nearly three years now.

David is an active participant in the OLSB Community forum and a member of the Community Council, which he considers as an opportunity to provide feedback and input into the development of the platform.

Table of Contents

Preface

You're probably reading this either because you have a small business, a hobby, a cause you care about deeply, a special interest, or a charitable organization that you want the whole world to know about. And what better way to publicize it than by building a website for it?

But let's face it: building and maintaining a good website is expensive. Professional web designers cost you a fortune. So, what's the way out?

One option is to build a website yourself. To build a website, you must know HTML—the language of web pages. And mind you, that's just the beginning. If you want a slick, modern website, you'll need at least a passing acquaintance with CSS, JavaScript, XML, SQL, and other such technologies.

Can you learn these technologies? Sure, you can. Visit your local Barnes and Noble, and you'll find several shelves filled with books that teach these technologies to everyone imaginable—novices, professionals, experts, smart people, geeks, nerds, dummies, idiots, teenagers, women, seniors, busy people, lazy people, you name it. You have an option of learning these technologies within time frames ranging from a mere five minutes to as long as a month. Once you select your gender, age, IQ, and the time that you want to spend on your endeavour, you can find the exact book for your requirements.

However, the question is: *Do you really want to immerse yourself in these technologies?* If you'd rather concentrate on doing more of whatever it is that you do for a living, than keeping abreast of differences in document object models of Firefox and Internet Explorer (whatever that means), this book is for you. It shows you how to build your own website without learning HTML or any other technology with those three and four-letter acronyms.

If you're wondering how you'd build a website without HTML, relax. This book is not about witchcraft. Your website will, of course, be built with HTML. But you won't be the one writing the HTML. Office Live Small Business will do it for you.

About Office Live Small Business

Office Live Small Business is Microsoft's web-presence service for small businesses. It's part software and part service. In fact, Microsoft calls this strategy **Software + Services**.

The software component consists of several useful online business programs and tools. Among them is a set of templating tools for building and managing websites. The tools ask you to fill in some information about your business, choose a few options for deciding the look and feel of your website, and ask you to write the text of the pitch that you wish to make to your visitors. Based on the information you provide, the tools generate a website for you.

The services component provides domain name management, web hosting, storage, and other infrastructural facilities required to maintain a website. Office Live Small Business bundles all these services in a single convenient package. Together, the two components help you build a website quickly and easily.

Sounds improbable? Let me give you an example that you'll easily relate to. There's a good chance that you use accounting software, such as QuickBooks, to balance your books. Did you have to take a crash course in accounting before you began using it? No. All you probably did was fill out a questionnaire about your business, set up a list of people who pay you money, and a list of people you pay money to, entered your bank account numbers, and then began recording daily transactions. That's it! Now your accounting software figures out the debits and credits. It decides whether an entry goes to your balance sheet or your income statement, and also generates balancing entries when you cancel a transaction. In fact, it performs all the accounting summersaults that are necessary to produce the pretty reports that help you prove your honesty to the IRS at the end of the year.

If you think about it, the goal of the entire exercise was to produce those pretty reports. You had the option of hiring an accountant, learning accounting yourself, or buying accounting software to achieve that goal. You chose the latter, in all likelihood, because it didn't cost as much as an accountant and didn't take up as much time as learning to balance the books yourself. That left you more time to do what you do best: run your business.

What QuickBooks does for your accounting, Office Live Small Business does for your website. Using its site-building tools, you can build an attractive website for yourself without learning any new technology. You can have your proverbial cake and eat it too. Moreover, the icing on the cake is that your site won't cost you a red cent; all you pay for is your domain name.

Is Office Live Small Business right for you?

That depends on many factors. Let me be brutally honest at the very outset. Just as your accounting software can't handle every imaginable accounting trick, Office Live Small Business doesn't have the tools to support every conceivable website feature.

If your goal is to build an informative yet great-looking website on a shoestring, if promoting your business means more to you than animations on your web pages, and if you want to build a website on which visitors can find the desired information quickly, easily, and intuitively; then Office Live Small Business is just what the doctor prescribed.

If, on the other hand, your goal is to build a website that's a collection of the coolest, slickest, flashiest, and most glamorous features from 73 of your most favourite websites; if the animations and special effects on your web pages mean more to you than the message they convey; if you'd rather use your site as a social networking vehicle rather than as a business promotion tool; then Office Live Small Business is not for you. Your only options are to hire a professional or learn all the necessary technologies yourself.

The bottom line is that you can't build the next Google, Facebook, or Amazon.com with Office Live Small Business. But as long as you keep your expectations in perspective, you can definitely build a website that will be the object of envy for your friends and competitors alike.

About this book

If it's so darn simple to build a website with Office Live Small Business, you might want to know why you need to buy this book. Allow me to tell you.

This book doesn't teach you *how* to hammer the proverbial nail; it tells you *why* the nail is required at all and *where* it should go.

You'll find tips, tricks, warnings, and bits of advice at every step. They'll help you avoid potential pitfalls and help you build a robust, consistent website that works well across browsers and operating systems.

The advice in this book is not random advice about web design; it's specific to designing websites with Office Live Small Business. It helps you optimize Office Live Small Business's settings to make full use of its potential.

If you're more adventurous, this book shows you how you can work around some of Office Live Small Business's limitations. I'm afraid you'll have to learn bits and pieces of those dreadful three and four-letter technologies, but I'll introduce them strictly on a need-to-know basis.

How to use this book

This book is not for bedside reading; it's a hands-on instruction manual. It's meant to be read sequentially. You'll get the most out of it if you build your website step-by-step as you read it from end-to-end. If this is your first attempt with building a website with Office Live Small Business, that would be the natural progression for you.

If you already have an Office Live Small Business website, you might be tempted to read random sections of this book to tweak your website. Random tweaking is a surefire recipe for making a complete mess of your website. Therefore, I strongly recommend against doing so. Of course, you don't have to throw away what you already have, but I recommend that you start your tweaking process with Chapter 1. As someone who's already familiar with Office Live Small Business, you'll be able to zip through the book at a faster clip than first-timers.

What this book covers

In Chapter 1: *Getting Started*, you'll learn the ABCs of Office Live Small Business and then go on a whirlwind tour of its site-building tools. Before calling it a day, you'll preview the starter site that Office Live Small Business creates for you to give you a head start on your project.

In Chapter 2: *Customizing Headers and Footers*, you'll start using the design tools you previewed in Chapter 1 to personalize your site's headers and footers. You'll customize its name and slogan, and in the bargain put your distinctive stamp on your website.

Chapter 3: *Setting Design Options* will help you decide the look and feel of your site. Which font should you use? What color scheme should you use? How should you lay out the site's navigation? It's quite easy to implement such important decisions with Office Live Small Business's design tools. This chapter will show you how.

Chapter 4: *Setting Page Display Options* will help you in deciding the structure of individual pages on your site. How wide will your web pages be? What kind of background will they have? How do you tweak design elements on your web pages? This chapter deals with these and other such questions.

By the time you're done with Chapter 5: *Building Your Website's Skeleton*, you'll have mastered Office Live Small Business's design tools. Have you ever seen a website that doesn't have a home page? I don't think so. No matter what business you are in, your website will need a few simple pages such as a Home page and a Contact Us page. These pages form the core around which you build the rest of the site. In this chapter, you'll build such a core. By the time you work your way through it, you'll have a four-page website—content and all.

In Chapter 6: *Building the Information Page*, you'll build upon the core you built in Chapter 5, and add pages that inform and educate the visitor about your products and services. You'll also learn how to work with text and images in formatting web pages.

Chapter 7: *Improving the Presentation* will show you how presentational aids such as tables, maps, slide shows, and hyperlinks help you present information in a more presentable and digestible format. Web pages that merely contain text and pictures are rather monotonous. Thankfully, several of these presentational aids are built right into Office Live Small Business's design tools. This chapter shows you how to leverage them.

In Chapter 8: *Fine-tuning the Design*, you'll continue to refine your website. You'll learn how to make your site friendlier to visitors by fine-tuning its navigation. You'll learn how to add your logo to your website in order to emphasize your brand. Finally, you'll learn how to tweak some of the settings you've chosen so far by customizing your website's stylesheet.

Chapter 9: *Venturing Beyond the Basics* will help you try your hand at writing your own HTML mark up to tweak your site. Office Live Small Business's built-in design tools make site-building point-and-click easy. But if you know HTML, the language of web pages, you can go where no Office Live Design Tool has gone before. Office Live Small Business is an extensible platform: it is possible to install off-the-shelf components to enhance your website. How to go about is the next skill you'll learn in this chapter. You'll install a custom FAQ component because the built-in FAQ page doesn't work as advertised.

In Chapter 10: *Optimizing for Search Engines*, you'll learn how to get your website noticed on Google and other search engines. You'll also get some straight talk on Search Engine Optimization that will help you understand how this much (ab)used term relates to the success of your website.

Appendix A: *Signing Up: Opening a New Office Live Small Business Account* covers the process of opening a new Office Live Small Business account.

Appendix B: *Setting Up E-mail Accounts* will teach you about setting up e-mail accounts.

Appendix C: *Submitting Your Site to Search Engines* teaches you about how to submit your site to search engines.

Appendix D: *Backup and Restore: Recovering from Disasters* elaborates on backing up and restoring data on the website.

Appendix E: *Reports: Analyzing Visitor Statistics* elaborates on the process of generating reports by analyzing visitor statistics.

Appendix F: *Answers to Pop Quizes* contains the answers to all pop quizes, chapter-wise.

What you need for this book

It doesn't take much to get started with Office Live Small Business. You'll find Microsoft's official system requirements for Office Live Small Business at http://smallbusiness. officelive.com/Support/SystemRequirements. But here's a simplified checklist of what you'll need:

1. A computer: You'll need a computer, of course. It can be either be a PC or an Apple Macintosh.

2. If it's a PC it should be running some edition of Windows XP, Windows Vista, or Windows 7. Windows 2003 Server or later will be fine too.

3. If it's a Mac, it should be running Mac OSX.

    Your computer doesn't have to be absolutely the latest and greatest model in the market. As long as you're happy with its speed and performance, you'll do just fine. The only stated hardware requirement Office Live Small Business has is a Super VGA (800 X 600), or higher-resolution display. Unless your monitor is an eighties-era relic, it should easily meet this requirement.

4. A browser: Office Live Small Business's tools are browser-based. So you'll need a browser too. If you have a PC, you have a choice of browsers: Internet Explorer 6 or later, or Mozilla Firefox 1.5 or later. If you have a Mac, you're limited to using only Mozilla Firefox. And no, Safari won't do.

5. Although Mozilla Firefox appears in Office Live Small Business's list of compatible browsers, I recommend using Internet Explorer if you have a PC. Some web design tools, such as the **Image Uploader**, work much better with Internet Explorer than they do with Mozilla Firefox. With a Mac, you have no choice but to use Mozilla Firefox.

6. An Internet Connection: It goes without saying that you'll need an Internet connection. When you build your website, you'll send large volumes of data to Office Live Small Business's web servers. So a broadband connection, such as a DSL or a cable connection, is recommended. You might be able to make do with a dial-up connection if that's the only option you have, but there are no guarantees.

7. An Office Live Small Business Account: Finally, you'll need an Office Live Small Business account. If you already have one, well and good. If you don't, turn to Appendix A (page 201), where you'll find step-by-step instructions on signing up for the service.

Who this book is for

This book is for small-business owners who want to build and customize their business websites on Microsoft's free-to-use platform. No technical knowledge is required.

Conventions

In this book, you will find a number of styles of text that distinguish between different kinds of information. Here are some examples of these styles, and an explanation of their meaning.

New terms and **important words** are shown in bold. Words that you see on the screen, in menus or dialog boxes for example, appear in the text like this: "clicking the Next button moves you to the **next** screen".

Code words in text are shown as follows: "The `<strong>` and `</strong>` in the markup you just tried out is tag pair."

A block of code will be set as follows:

```
<strong>Welcome to my web site.</strong>
```

> Warnings or important notes appear in a box like this.

> Tips and tricks appear like this.

Practical, hands-on actions and instructions are introduced with a Time for action heading, and use numbered steps to make the text easier to read:

Time for action – uploading a document

1. Action 1

2. Action 2

3. Action 3

When instructions need some extra explanation so that they make sense, they are followed with...

What just happened?

... which explains how the task or instructions you just completed work, so that you learn how Office Live Small Business works as you complete the steps.

You will also find some other learning aids in the book, including:

Pop quiz

These are short multiple choice questions intended to help you test your own understanding.

Have a go hero

These set practical challenges and give you ideas for experimenting with what you have learned.

Reader feedback

Feedback from our readers is always welcome. Let us know what you think about this book—what you liked or may have disliked. Reader feedback is important for us to develop titles that you really get the most out of.

To send us general feedback, simply send an email to feedback@packtpub.com, and mention the book title via the subject of your message.

If there is a book that you need and would like to see us publish, please send us a note in the **SUGGEST A TITLE** form on www.packtpub.com or email suggest@packtpub.com.

If there is a topic that you have expertise in and you are interested in either writing or contributing to a book on, see our author guide on www.packtpub.com/authors.

Customer support

Now that you are the proud owner of a Packt book, we have a number of things to help you to get the most from your purchase.

Companion Website

This book has a companion website, www.officeliveguide.com. I've built it with Office Live Small Business as I wrote this book. The screenshots in the book will look familiar if you browse the companion website as you work your way through the book.

Unlike most desktop programs you install on your computer, Office Live Small Business is an online service. Naturally, there will be bug fixes and minor enhancements from time to time. The companion website will track these changes for you and provide instructions on using the new features.

The website also features bonus content, tutorials, and as well as the tools and downloads referenced in the book.

Errata

Although we have taken every care to ensure the accuracy of our content, mistakes do happen. If you find a mistake in one of our books—maybe a mistake in the text or the code—we would be grateful if you would report this to us. By doing so, you can save other readers from frustration, and help us to improve subsequent versions of this book. If you find any errata, please report them by visiting `http://www.packtpub.com/support`, selecting your book, clicking on the **let us know** link, and entering the details of your errata. Once your errata are verified, your submission will be accepted and the errata added to any list of existing errata. Any existing errata can be viewed by selecting your title from `http://www.packtpub.com/support`.

Piracy

Piracy of copyright material on the Internet is an ongoing problem across all media. At Packt, we take the protection of our copyright and licenses very seriously. If you come across any illegal copies of our works, in any form, on the Internet, please provide us with the location address or website name immediately so that we can pursue a remedy.

Please contact us at `copyright@packtpub.com` with a link to the suspected pirated material.

We appreciate your help in protecting our authors, and our ability to bring you valuable content.

Questions

You can contact us at `questions@packtpub.com` if you are having a problem with any aspect of the book, and we will do our best to address it.

1
Getting Started

Office Live Small Business is quite a feature-rich product. Website-building tools make up only a small part of its overall feature set. Not only that, those tools are scattered over several web pages. Therefore, it's a good idea to get oriented so that you can find your bearings quickly once we start building your website in earnest.

In this chapter, you will:

- Learn how to sign in and sign out of your Office Live Small Business account
- Preview a four-page starter website that Office Live Small Business automatically creates for you
- Explore the site-building tools at your disposal and learn to navigate between them

Important preliminary points

Have you already signed up for Office Live Small Business? If not, now's the time.

You don't need to have a domain name to sign up and start creating your website. In fact, Office Live Small Business's sign-up process doesn't even ask you for one. It assigns a third-level domain alias to your website instead. After you build your site, and if you like it, you can register a domain name of your choice with a registrar of your choice and associate it with your website.

For example, when I opened an Office Live Small Business account for this book's companion website, I hadn't decided on a domain name. I just opened a new Office Live Small Business account and was assigned `officeliveguide.web.officelive.com` as the third-level domain name for my website. After I built the website, I registered the domain name `officeliveguide.com` and associated it with my website.

I recommend that you do the same. That way, you won't have to go through the hassle of changing registrars if you don't like your Office Live Small Business website.

Instructions for registering a new domain name for your website as well as instructions for pointing an existing domain name at your website are on the companion website at www.officeliveguide.com/domain.aspx.

Signing in

Let's start with signing in to your Office Live Small Business account.

Time for action – sign in to your Office Live Small Business account

1. Browse to www.officelive.com. The **Microsoft Office Live** web page appears:

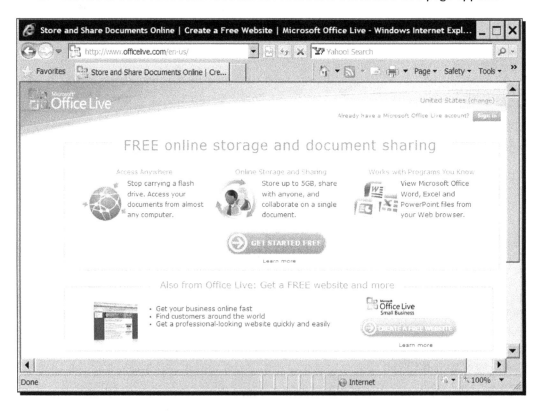

2. Click the **Sign in** button in the top right-hand corner. You'll arrive at Office Live Small Business's **Sign In** page, as shown in the following screenshot:

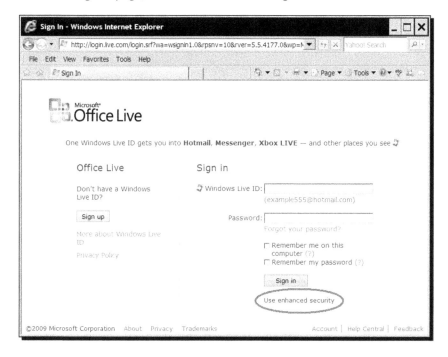

3. If you prefer a secured sign-in, as I do, click the **Use enhanced security** link under the **Sign in** button and Office Live Small Business will display a secured sign-in page. The secured page looks just like the unsecured page. But if you look carefully, the link under the **Sign in** button now reads **Use standard security**.

When you use the secured sign-in, your Windows Live ID and password are encrypted when they're sent over the wire for authentication. This prevents the bad guys from stealing them. That's why online stores, bank websites, or any other websites that require you to provide sensitive information use secured channels. Unlike your banking session, however, Office Live only uses the secured connection for signing you in. Once you're in, it reverts to the standard connection.

4. Enter your Windows Live ID and password.

5. If you want Office Live Small Business to remember your Windows Live ID, select the **Remember me on this computer** checkbox.

6. If you want Office Live Small Business to remember your password as well, select the **Remember my password** checkbox below it.

Remember me on this computer and **Remember my password** checkboxes make signing in easier in the future. But once you select them both, anybody who has access to your computer account can access your Office Live Small Business account as well. In fact, that person will have access to all of your Microsoft accounts; such as Windows Live, Windows Live Spaces, and Office Live Mail, which are secured by your Windows Live ID. Personally, I prefer to enter my credentials every time I visit a website.

7. Click the **Sign in** button. You'll arrive at the **Microsoft Office Live Home** page:

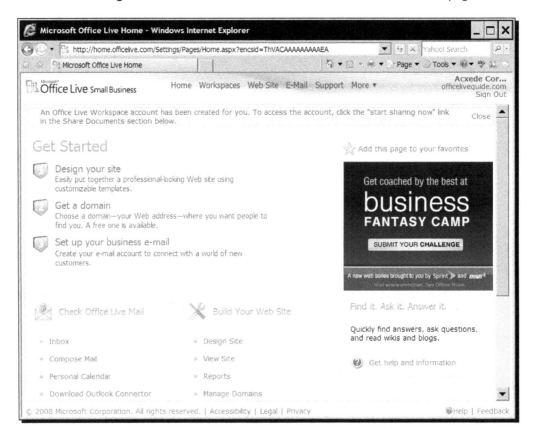

What just happened?

You signed in to your Office Live Small Business account and arrived at the **Microsoft Office Live Home** page. That's too long a name to repeat throughout the remainder of this book. So, I'll simply call it the **Home** page. But don't confuse it with the home page of the website you'll soon build. We'll call that page the Default page for reasons that I'll explain in Chapter 5.

The **Home** page is your dashboard for managing your Office Live Small Business account. It sports one-click access to several common tasks that you're likely to perform after signing-in to your account.

But the page is a bit confusing for three reasons:

- ◆ It has too many links.
- ◆ Many of the links are redundant. For example, there are three links on the page that lead to the website section.
- ◆ Although the page is clearly for the benefit of first-time visitors, you see it every time you sign in to your Office Live Small Business account.

But with time, you'll learn to use this page to work more efficiently. The links we'll focus on for now are in the site navigation bar at the top centre of the page: **Home**, **Workspaces**, **Web Site**, **E-mail**, **Support**, and **More**. You'll see these links on almost every page. They represent Office Live Small Business's top-level functions. Each link leads you to a section of the site—a sub-site of sorts, which focuses on that particular function.

Although we'll spend most of our time in the website section, which deals with building and maintaining your website, we'll briefly touch upon other sections, such as the **E-mail** section and a few sub-sections under **More**, when necessary.

Signing out

Now that you know how to sign in, the next logical step is to learn how to sign out.

Time for action – sign out of your Office Live Small Business account

1. Click the **Sign Out** link in the top right-hand corner of the **Home** page. You'll find this link on almost all pages under your account. Office Live Small Business will inform you that you've signed out.

2. Close your browser.

What just happened?

You signed out of your Office Live Small Business account. You could simply have closed the browser window, but that's not really prudent.

Whenever you sign in, the Windows Live ID authentication system stores some information in browser cookies so that you don't have to sign in repeatedly. Closing the browser window doesn't get rid of the cookies. So, anyone who uses your computer after you, has full access to all your accounts attached to your Windows Live ID. When you sign out explicitly, as you just did, the cookies are deleted and others can't access your account accidentally.

Another benefit of logging off, and thereby deleting the cookies, is that your computer doesn't "remember" anything from your previous session.

Exploring the website section

The website section of your account contains the tools you'll use to build your website. Let's visit the section and get familiar with them.

Time for action – exploring the website section of your account

1. Sign in to your account.

2. On the **Home** page, click the **Web Site** link in the site navigation bar. The **Page Manager** page appears.

Page Manager: the site-management tool

The **Page Manager** page you're looking at, is your website's management console. It's your dashboard for building and managing your website. As it's the first page you see when you come to the **Web Site** section, it's the logical place to initiate actions. You'll spend a great deal of time on it. Therefore, let's explore it in detail.

When the page first loads, the element that really catches your attention is the upside-down tab titled **Get started with your own Web site**. It's also the least relevant element. You'll find this tab on several Office Live Small Business pages. It mostly sports links to help topics. You can collapse it and maximize your work area by clicking the **Hide Getting Started** link. Go ahead, try it.

The starter website

"Well, that's really nice", you're probably thinking, "but where do I make a web page"? That's what the little toolbar in the middle of the page and the links underneath it are for. We'll get to them in just a few minutes, trust me! But first, let's take a quick look at a little surprise that Office Live Small Business has in store for you: a starter website.

Time for action – viewing the starter website

1. Click the **View Site** link (or the icon next to it) on the blue toolbar that spans the middle of the page. A new window opens displaying a skeletal, but fully functional website:

Your starter site may look slightly different if you scrutinize it minutely. But for practical purposes, it will have all of the design elements that you see in the image above.

2. Click the links in the navigation bar to view different pages on the website.

3. Close the preview window.

What just happened?

Office Live Small Business automatically creates a skeleton site with four sample pages when you sign up for the service. You just previewed that site.

We'll use this site to dig deeper into Office Live Small Business's features and tools. Then we'll use some of the pages to practice the common tasks that you'll perform while building and maintaining your website.

Notice that you don't see any advertisements when you view your website. Office Live Small Business is an ad-supported service but it displays advertisements only on your account management console. Therefore, you only see them when you're building your site. Visitors to your finished website will not see them. This feature alone sets Microsoft Office Live Small Business apart from other site-building tools. A *free website* is exactly that—no strings attached.

More about Page Manager

Let's now get back to exploring the **Page Manager**.

It's made up of the following components, as you can see in the partial screenshot above:

◆ The table of pages at the bottom displays a row for every page on your website, along with a few options to manipulate it. It also displays the size of the page and the date when you changed it last.

◆ The **Page Manager** toolbar that spans the page, just above the page list, houses links for performing common site-maintenance tasks. In fact, you just clicked on the **View Site** link to preview the starter website.

◆ The **Site actions** tile, in the top right-hand corner, which is a pull-down menu with options for performing site-maintenance tasks that you don't need to perform all that often.

Time for action – viewing page properties

1. Click the **Properties** link for the **About Us** page; it's the third link in the options column of the page list. The **Choose page properties** window opens:

2. Take a minute to explore the two tabs and read the information on them.

What just happened?

You just explored the properties of a web page.

One of the most important properties of a page is its title. It appears in the browser's title bar when the page opens in a visitor's browser. When a visitor bookmarks the page or creates a shortcut for it on his desktop, its name is set to the title of the web page. That way, people can find a given page among their bookmarks or shortcuts quite easily.

Look at the following web page, for example:

The title of the page above is **Home**. That's not very helpful. If you change the title to something like **The Office Live Guide—Home Page**, people can find the page easily among their bookmarks or shortcuts.

Search engines attach a good deal of importance to a page's title. It appears as the primary link for that page in search results. More significantly, the title plays a big role in how search engines determine how to index the page. If the title is simply **Home**, it could end up in some category related to home ownership, homes for the elderly, or even funeral homes. But **The Office Live Guide—Home Page** tells the **spiders** that the page has something to do with Office Live and they can index it accordingly.

What's a spider?

A spider is a little program that a search engine uses to traverse websites and index their content. Each search engine has its own spider. It follows links from page to page as it finds them. This process of following links is called **crawling**.

Spiders are also called **crawlers** or **bots**. The celebrity among bots, of course, is **Googlebot**—Google's spider.

Of course, the title is not the sole criterion spiders use to index your pages but it plays a significant enough role in their decisions for you to take the trouble of giving meaningful titles to your web pages.

The information on the Search Engine Optimization tab describes meta tags which help search engines index your web site. We'll explore search engines and meta tags in Chapter 10. In the mean time, can you think of three words or phrases that best describe your small business? Write them down in the space below.

1. _____

2. _____

3. _____

If nothing comes to your mind right away, that's okay. But put the task on your to-do list. Remember, you're going to need them in Chapter 10.

Have a go hero – explore page properties

At this stage, you don't have to understand what each piece of information or each setting means. I just want you to get accustomed to the lingo of web pages and browse around, so that you get an overview of a web page's properties from 30,000 feet. We'll get back to the details as we progress with building your website.

Try clicking the **Edit navigation position** button. A new **Navigation** window opens. Read the instructions in the window and then close it.

When you're done exploring the page properties, click **Cancel** to return to the **Page Manager**.

Site Designer and Page Editor: the design tools

Some design elements of a website apply to the site as a whole; others apply only to a specific web page. For example, the title of your website, usually the name of your business, appears on every web page of your site. The text on the **Home** page, on the other hand, is specific only to that page; it's not relevant anywhere else. Office Live Small Business has two distinct tools to manipulate each category of settings. The tool for manipulating site-wide settings is called the **Site Designer** and the tool for manipulating settings on individual pages is called the **Page Editor**.

Time for action – exploring Site Designer

1. Pull down the **Design Site** menu from the Page Manager toolbar and select the first option, **Design site**, as shown in the following screenshot:

2. A new window opens, displaying the **Microsoft Office Live Small Business Web Design Tool** web page. It has two tabs: **Site Designer** and **Page Editor**. The **Site Designer** tab is active when the window opens, as shown in the following screenshot:

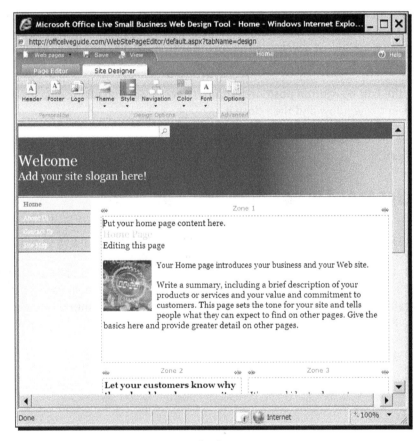

3. You've seen this page before; it's the homepage of your starter website. But notice that this time around, there's Microsoft Office 2007-style ribbon at the top. The buttons on the ribbon that have small black triangles at the bottom are pull-down selection menus. The buttons that don't have the triangles open property windows like the one you saw while viewing page properties earlier in this chapter. Let's try changing a setting to get an idea of how the **Site Designer** settings work.

4. Click on the **Header** button on the ribbon. The **Customize Header** window, as shown in the next screenshot, opens.

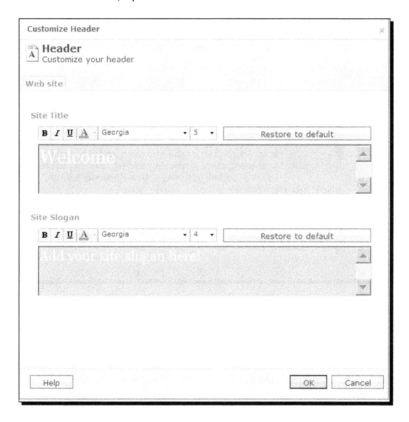

5. Change the text **Welcome** in the gray box in the **Site Title** section to **Welcome to my site**. Click **OK**. The window closes.

6. Notice that the **Site Title** on the web page displayed in **Site Designer** is now **Welcome to my site**. Click the **View** link just above the **Site Designer** tab. A dialog box opens to ask you whether you want to save your changes. Click **OK**.

7. The dialog box goes away and a new browser window opens with a preview of your starter website. Notice that the title of the website is now **Welcome to my site**:

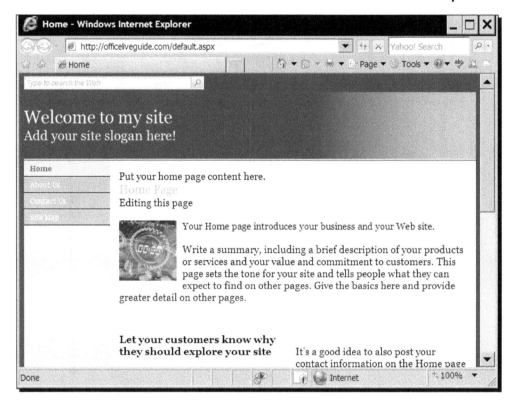

8. Click on the navigation links on the left-hand side to view other pages on the website. You'll see that the new title appears on all the pages.

9. Close the preview window and return to **Site Designer**.

10. Close the **Site Designer** window and return to **Page Manager**.

Have a go hero – explore Site Designer's ribbon

Go back to **Site Designer** and try clicking on the various buttons on its ribbon. Every time you click a button, a pull-down menu or a small window will appear. The menus and window will give you a sense of the kind of site-wide settings available in Office Live Small Business.

Don't worry if you don't understand what they are for. Right now, your goal is to get an overview of the tools at your disposal from 30,000 feet.

When you're done, return to the **Page Manager**.

Time for action – exploring Page Editor

1. Pull down the **Design Site** menu from the **Page Manager** toolbar and select the second option, **Edit pages**.

2. The **Microsoft Office Live Small Business Web Design Tool** opens, once again, in a new window. But this time, the **Page Editor** tab is the active tab when the window opens, as shown in the following screenshot:

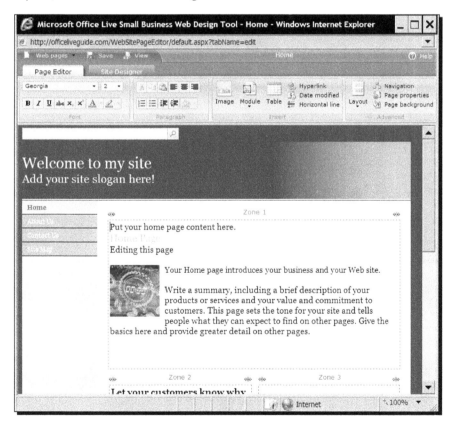

3. The **Page Editor**, too, has a Microsoft Office 2007-style ribbon. The buttons and links on the ribbon, however, will remind you of a word processor. And for good reason, **Page Editor** is primarily a tool for editing a web page's content. The content on web pages resides in zones that are marked by red dotted lines around them.

4. Let us try doing something simple in the **Page Editor**. Select the first line in **Zone 1**, one that reads **Put your home page content here.**, the same way that you'd select text in a word processor.

5. Click the **B** button on the ribbon, the first button in the bottom row of the ribbon's **Font** section, to make the text bold.

6. Click the **Save** button in the top left-hand corner of the window; it is just above the **Page Editor** tab.

7. Click the **View** button next to it to preview the site. Notice that the text now appears in bold typeface.

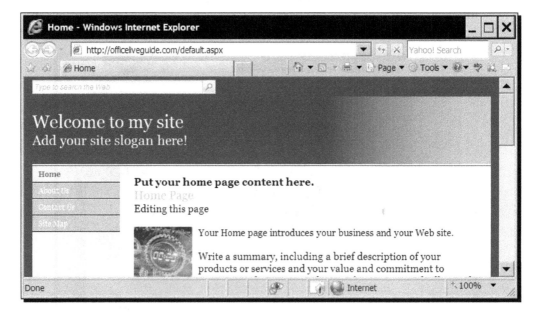

8. Click on the navigation links on the left-hand side to view other pages on the website. You'll see that the text on other pages hasn't changed. That's because making the text bold is an action specific to the **Home** page. It has no bearing on the content of the other pages.

9. Close the preview window and return to **Page Editor**.

10. Close the **Site Designer** window and return to **Page Manager**.

What just happened?

The two primary tools for designing your website with Office Live Small Business are **Site Designer** and **Page Editor**. You just got a bird's eye view of each. To recap:

1. **Site Designer** is the tool for setting design options that affect the entire website.
2. **Page Editor** is the tool for designing and editing content on individual web pages.

Although you're not quite ready to be a professional web designer just yet, you should now have a pretty good idea of what's involved in building a website using Office Live Small Business.

Have a go hero – explore Page Editor's ribbon

Open up **Page Editor** and try the options available on its ribbon. That should give you a general idea of the range of page-design options available to you.

Some of them will be Greek to you. Fear not. We'll figure them out as we progress.

When you're done, return to the **Page Manager**.

Pop quiz 1.1

1. To open the **Home** page in **Page Editor**, you chose the **Edit pages** option on the **Design Site** pull-down menu on **Page Manager**'s toolbar. Can you think of another way to do the same thing?

    Hint: Look carefully at the Page Manager's page list.

     Remember: answers to Pop quizzes are in Appendix A to discourage you from cheating!

2. Open the **Home** page in the **Page Editor** in any way that you want to. Now, how would you bring up the **About Us** page in the **Page Editor** without going back to the **Page Manager**?

    Hint: Look for a link or a button in the top half of the Page Editor window.

The rest of the tools: the galleries

In addition to the **Page Manager**, the **Site Designer**, and the **Page Editor**, Office Live Small Business has three additional tools: **Image Gallery**, **Document Gallery**, and **Template Gallery**. You can access them by clicking on the links in the navigation pane on **Page Manager**'s left-hand side, as shown in the following screenshot:

The **Image Gallery** contains a set of tools for editing and uploading pictures to your website. We'll see the precise mechanics of doing so in Chapter 7. For now, just remember that any picture that appears on your website will reside here.

The **Document Gallery** contains tools to upload downloadable documents and other special purpose files to your website. Again, we'll see how to do this in Chapter 7. At this point, it's sufficient to remember that downloadable documents such as brochures and price lists belong in the **Document Gallery**.

The **Template Gallery** is a tool to manage web page templates. Templates are boilerplate designs for web pages. Office Live Small Business provides a selection of professionally-designed templates right out of the box. But you can also build custom templates of your own design. We'll see how to build them and store them in the Template gallery in Chapter 5.

The fourth link, **Reports,** leads you to a set of web analytics tools. Web analytics tools analyze the traffic to your website. They help you understand who's visiting your site and why. But they don't play a role in the building of the website, per se.

Have a go hero – explore the galleries

Go back to the **Page Manager** and click on each of the links in the left navigation pane, in turn, to briefly visit the sections that they lead to. Notice that the first three sections are empty and have the same links in their left navigation panes as the **Page Manager**. The **Reports** section, on the other hand, displays some content and has a different set of links.

To return to the **Page Manager** from the **Image Gallery**, for example, you can simply click the **Web Site** link at the top of the left navigation pane, but to return to **Page Manager** from **Reports**, you'll have to click the **Web Site** link in the site navigation bar.

Summary

In this chapter, I gave you a whirlwind tour of Office Live Small Business's site-building tools. Of course, we didn't dig deeply into any of them. But that wasn't the idea anyway. The goal of this chapter was to give you an overall sense of what you're getting into!

Here's a recap of the chapter:

- ◆ Office Live Small Business has a set of tools for building a website. You can access them by signing in to your Office Live Small Business account.

- ◆ When you sign up, Office Live Small Business automatically creates a four-page starter website for you.

- ◆ **Page Manager** is the dashboard for managing your website.

- ◆ The primary site-building tools are the **Site Designer** and the **Page Editor**.

- ◆ **Site Designer** is used for setting site-wide design elements.

- ◆ **Page Editor** is used for editing the content of individual web pages.

- ◆ A set of three ancillary tools: **Image Gallery**, **Document Gallery**, and **Template Gallery** is useful in storing and manipulating pictures, downloadable documents, and page templates, respectively.

That's just about everything you'll need to know to get started. In the next chapter, we'll jump right in and start building your very own website!

2
Customizing Headers and Footers

Although a website is just a collection of web pages, the collection is not random. A central theme ties the web pages together with common elements such as branding, logo, layout, and formatting. On really large websites, the interweaving of these elements can be quite complex. Each of Google's websites, for example, has its distinct identity and yet you can identify it as a "Google website". It takes a small army of designers and illustrators to achieve such a "Similar But Distinct" identity.

But it's fairly easy to establish a unifying theme for the web pages of a small website, such as yours. And you can do it all by yourself; a common header and footer is all that's usually necessary. Naturally, it would make immense sense if you could design a template for headers and footers once and use it on all of your web pages.

A template isn't all that revolutionary a concept. You've probably built a template in your word processor for your letterhead or for a boilerplate, for example. Many widely-used applications save you the trouble of repetitive formatting by allowing you to make templates. Therefore, it shouldn't come as a great surprise to you that you can build page templates in Office Live Small Business as well.

A web page template in Office Live Small Business has two components: information and design. The information component consists of the text and images that are specific to your website, such as your company name, logo, slogan, copyright notice, and so on. The design component deals with choosing the right font, colors, background pictures, and other such visual elements. Once you configure the necessary settings, you'll have a shell, so to say, which will appear around the content on your web pages.

You'll start building the shell in this chapter and shape it to perfection over the course of the next two chapters. In this chapter, you will:

- Decide what your website's title should be, and set it in your template
- Decide what your website's slogan should be, and set it in your template
- Decide what information should go into your website's footer, and set it

We'll deal with the design and page layout elements of the shell in the next two chapters.

Choosing a title for your website

A website's title is usually the name of the business it represents. My little company is called *Acxede*, for example. Therefore, it's logical that my site's title mimics my company's name. Now, there's only so much real estate available on a web page for the title. Because Acxede happens to be a short name, it can fit into most page layouts. But if your business is incorporated as *Anthony Donaldson's Vacuum Cleaner Sales, Service, and Rentals Incorporated*, this scheme of things breaks down. What do you do then? A good rule of thumb is to echo whatever name is on your business card. Unless your business card is the size of a postcard, you'd have shortened the name to something like *Anthony Donaldson Inc.* Use that as your site's title.

People often want to set their domain name as their site's title. Because my company is called *Acxede*, it would, of course, be terrific to have *acxede.com* as my domain name. And I do. Unfortunately, not everyone is that lucky. More likely than not, the domain name you want is already taken. Let's say that you're Sam and you own a deli called, naturally, *Sam's Deli*. Everyone just calls it "Sam's". It wouldn't be unreasonable for you to want the domain name *sams.com*. The trouble is that Sam's Publishing has already snapped it up. Okay, so how about *samsdeli.com*? Nope. Another Sam owns it. So you're forced to settle for a domain name that doesn't echo the name of your business; something like *samsfreshfood.com*, perhaps. Nevertheless, your website's title should still say "Sam's Deli" because that's the name of your business, no matter what domain name you ultimately settle on.

Now that you know more about setting a website's title than you ever wanted to, let's get around to doing the honors.

Time for action – setting the site title

1. Pull down the **Design Site** menu from the **Page Manager** toolbar and select **Design site**. A new window opens, displaying the **Microsoft Office Live Small Business Web Design Tool** web page with **Site Designer** as the active tab.

2. Click on the **Header** button on the ribbon. The **Customize Header** dialog opens.

3. Replace the text **Welcome to my site** in the gray box in the **Site Title** section with your site's title. I'm going to set it as **The Office Live Guide** for the site that I'm building—this book's companion site.

4. Pull down the select options for the font face just above the title. You'll see a choice of seven fonts: **Arial**, **Courier New**, **Georgia**, **Tahoma**, **Times New Roman**, **Trebuchet MS**, and **Verdana**.

   Why only seven? After all, Microsoft Word seems to have a hundred. The reason is that in the Web's architecture, the task of displaying a given font is delegated to your browser. Not every browser can display every font. If a browser can't display a font that you've specified, it displays one that it thinks is right. Such a substitution might distort your web page. But these seven fonts are, more or less, the least common denominator; most browsers support them. Therefore, the chances of your web pages being distorted are quite slim if you choose one of these seven.

   So which of these seven should you choose? Follow this two step process:

   ❑ If one of the fonts in the list looks like the font on your letterhead or the sign above your office, choose that one.

   ❑ Not even close? Choose either **Georgia** or **Verdana**.

   Most fonts, such as **Arial** or **Times New Roman**, came to computer displays from the world of print. They were designed to look good on paper. Making a font look good on paper is relatively easy because text is printed on paper in very high resolution. On a monitor, however, pixels of resolution are at a premium. Besides, the resolution can vary from monitor to monitor. Therefore, text will look better onscreen if you use fonts that are designed specifically for monitors rather than using fonts that are grandfathered from the print world. **Georgia** and **Verdana** are designed specifically for monitors and so they're the ideal candidates for the text on your web pages.

   Set the font you've chosen. I've set it to **Georgia**.

5. Next, pull down the adjacent select options for the font size. You'll see a choice of seven font sizes. They're conveniently numbered from **1** to **7**. Size **1** is the smallest and size **7** is the largest. For some inexplicable reason, people often choose a size that's either too big or too small. I recommend size **5** for the title. That's just about right for most websites built with Office Live Small Business.

One thing you've got to remember, though, is that: Thou shalt use Georgia or Verdana in size 5 for your site's title is **not** the eleventh commandment. I've suggested these settings because, in my experience, they are just about right for most websites built with Office Live Small Business. They make the header appear proportionate to the text on the web pages. But, they may not be right for your site if its title or slogan is either too long or too short. Come back and experiment with the font face or size of the header elements if your pages look out-of-whack after you finish building your website.

Set the font size you've chosen. I've set it to **5**.

6. Although you can choose a color for the title, let's skip it for now. The choice of color depends on other layout options as well. Therefore, we'll address it when we set the design and layout options in Chapter 3.

Although you can make the title bold, italicize it, or underline it, you'd do well by avoiding the temptation. Depending on a combination of factors such as the font face, font size, and resolution of a visitor's monitor, these special effects can make the text quite difficult to read. The last thing you want to do is to inadvertently make the title of your site unreadable.

7. Your **Customize Header** dialog should now look something like this:

8. Keep the window open; you might as well set a slogan for your website while you're there.

What just happened?

You just took the first baby steps towards building your website! Agreed, all you did was set the site title—not exactly the kind of stuff that you'd write home about, but it's a fine start nevertheless.

Your site's title and slogan, which you'll set in the following section, play an important role in helping people find your site from search engines.

Choosing a slogan for your website

An Office Live Small Business website's slogan is really just its tagline; so I'll use the terms interchangeably. Successful businesses use catchy taglines to reinforce their brands. What comes to mind when you hear "Just do it!"? Nike. How about "Don't Leave Home Without It"? American Express. And "Eat Fresh"? Subway, of course.

See? People subconsciously associate taglines with brands or products. Come to think of it, the whole point of building your website is to reinforce your brand. Naturally, a good tagline will go a long way towards achieving your goal.

While a tagline sounds like a no-brainer, not every business has one. If you don't, you're not alone. After all, you can't spend a few million dollars to come up with one the way Nike, American Express, and Subway probably did. But if you happen to have one, it's a good idea to immortalize it on your website. And if you don't, now's the time to scratch the creative side of your brain and think of one.

But don't despair if you can't. You may be able to substitute a description of your business for the tagline with good effect. If you've shortened *Anthony Donaldson's Vacuum Cleaner Sales, Service, and Rentals Incorporated*, to *Anthony Donaldson Inc.*, your tagline can be *Vacuum Cleaner Sales, Service, and Rentals*, or something to that effect. It may not be as potent as Nike's tagline, but at least it tells people what Anthony Donaldson does for a living.

Time for action – setting the site slogan

1. Replace the text **Add your site slogan here!** in the gray box in the **Site Slogan** section with your site slogan. I'm going to set it to **Build your own website in a day!**

2. Pull down the select options for the font face just above the title and set it to the font you've chosen. I'm setting it to **Georgia** again.

3. Next, pull down the adjacent select options for the font size and set it to **4**.

   Why **4**? I didn't pull the number **4** out of a hat. I chose it because size **4** is a size smaller than size **5**, the size of my site's title. If your **Site Title** is set to a size other than five, choose one size smaller than the size of your site's title.

4. As with the **Site Title**, don't select a color for your **Site Slogan**. We'll come back to it in Chapter 3, as promised. And stay away from the **B**, **I**, and **U** buttons as well. Your **Customize Header** dialog should now look something like this:

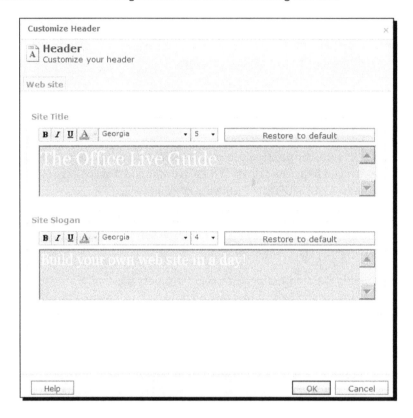

5. Click the **OK** button at the bottom of the **Customize Header** dialog. It closes and you arrive back at the **Site Designer**.

6. Click the **View** button in **Site Designer**.

You'll be using the **View** button, and the **Save** button next to it, quite often. When I want you to click the **Save** button, I'll simply tell you to save your work. If I want you to click the **View** button, I'll tell you to preview your website. Whenever I refer to these buttons, directly or indirectly, you now know where to find them.

7. A pop-up message asks you whether you want to save your changes. Click **OK**.

8. A preview of your site comes up in a new browser window. Notice that the site now displays the new title and slogan, as shown in the following screenshot:

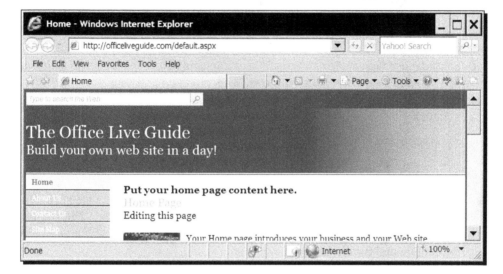

9. After you've admired your handiwork long enough, close the preview window and return to **Site Designer**.

What just happened?

You added a slogan to go along with your site's title. Why so much fuss about simply setting the title and slogan? In a word: *findability*.

 Findability? I didn't make that word up, by the way. Honest! Well-known web usability expert Jakob Nielsen did. A site is **findable** if it's easy to find; that is, it appears near the top of search engine results when a person searches for relevant terms. You can find great advice about building usable websites on Mr. Nielsen's website at `http://www.useit.com`.

Search engines attach considerable importance to the title of a web page. It tells them what the page is all about. But that's not the only thing they look at. They also try to determine whether the text on the web page has anything to do with its title. Because the slogan appears on every page with the title, a strong correlation between the two and their correlation with the text on your web pages will determine your web page's ranking in search results. To put it mildly, if your site's title and slogan stink, so will its ranking in the search results!

Therefore, don't take these settings lightly. If you don't put enough thought behind them, you risk relegating your web pages to obscurity.

Have a go hero – experiment with the site title and site slogan

Although I handed down the edicts on setting the font face and the font size for the **Site Title** and the **Site Slogan**, by no means are my recommendations cast in stone. Although following my recommendations will save you a good deal of time and heartache, you'll do a disservice to yourself if you don't experiment on your own. Depending on how long your **Site Title** or **Site Slogan** is, you might find a better combination of these settings if you try out a few variations. Here are a few suggestions:

♦ If you've set your font to **Georgia**, you might want to try **Verdana.**

♦ How about **Georgia** for the **Site Title** and **Verdana** for the **Site Slogan**? Or vice-versa?

♦ Although I've recommended that you set the font size for your **Site Slogan** a size smaller than the font size for your **Site Title**, you might want to try a font size two sizes smaller than the size for your **Site Title**, especially if you've set different fonts for the title and the slogan.

♦ **Verdana** is a wide font. If your site title or slogan has several wide letters like W and M, **Verdana** may not be the right choice. You might want to try a similar but narrower font, such as **Arial**.

Try out a few variations and settle on one that you like the best. You might want to get an opinion from a friend or a co-worker. And remember, you can come back and play with these settings any time.

Pop quiz 2.1

1. Which of the following attributes make your website more "findable"?

   A. Your site's header

   B. Your site's title

   C. Your site's font setting

   D. Your site's slogan

Setting the footer

Okay, so you now have your website's header under control. Let's jump to the other end of the page and deal with the footer. The usual suspects you'll find in the footers are:

♦ Navigation links that mimic at least some of a website's main navigation

♦ Contact information or a link to a page that displays contact information

♦ Copyright notice

♦ Links to privacy policy, disclaimers, and other fine print

 Why are these elements commonly found in the footer? Because people expect to find them in the footer. A basic principle in designing websites is to place information where people can find it easily. It's not against the law to put the copyright notice in the header. But if you do, people are not likely to find it.

It's a good idea to stick to conventional wisdom and include the following elements in your website's footer:

♦ A link to the **Contact Us** page because most people expect to find contact information in the footer

♦ A copyright notice to placate your lawyers

♦ A link to the privacy policy of your website because people often don't part with their e-mail addresses and are reluctant to contact you if your website doesn't have a privacy policy

So, your footer will look something like this:

And what about site navigation links? We won't consider them. Here's why:

♦ As you'll see shortly, you can't build elaborate footers with Office Live Small Business, like the ones you see on blogs these days. Site navigation links tend to clutter the available real estate.

♦ Their purpose in footers is to save people the trouble of having to scroll long web pages vertically simply to find a navigation link. Since you're building a small website with compact informational pages and not an online magazine with long articles, you don't really need them.

♦ Some websites use images or scripting languages to build site navigation. People who turn off images or scripting support in their browsers can't see such navigation links. Ten years ago, during the Web's Stone Age, some designers started placing text navigation links in the footers to accommodate those people. Like most modern site-building tools, Office Live Small Business generates text-only site navigation. So, you don't have to repeat the links in the footer.

But that said, you may feel that the navigation links do belong in your website's footer. In the coming sections of this chapter, I'll show you how to add the **Contact Us** and **Privacy Policy** links to the footer. Once you know the process, you'll be able to add any other links you wish.

Time for action – customizing the footer

1. Pull down the **Design Site** menu from the **Page Manager** toolbar and select **Design site**. The **Microsoft Office Live Small Business Web Design Tool** web page opens with **Site Designer** as the active tab.

2. Click on the **Footer** button on the ribbon. The **Customize your footer** window opens:

Your window may not look this squeaky clean; you might already have a few links in the **List of Links** and some text in the **Footer Text** box. If so, get rid of them. To remove a link, select a link in the **List of Links** and then click the **Remove** button. To banish the footer text, simply erase it as you would in a word processor.

3. Let's start by adding the **Contact Us** link. Click the **Add Link** button. The **Link Properties** dialog opens:

4. Type **Contact Us** in the **Link Name** text box. That's what the link will say on your web pages.

5. Type **/contactus.aspx** in the **Link Address** textbox. That's the address of the **Contact Us** page. Note that the link begins with a forward slash (/). It tells Office Live Small Business that the web page is on your website and not on some random website on the Web. If you forget the forward slash, the link won't work.

Wait a minute! Where did the address come from? Recall from Chapter 1 that every web page has **Properties**. You can view them by clicking the **Properties** link against the page in **Page Manager**. I just looked it up before I wrote the instructions for the previous step. Another way to find the address is to preview the web page. The text in the preview window's address bar, after the last forward slash (/), is the address. It's **contactus.aspx** in this case.

6. Click **OK**. The **Link Properties** dialog closes and you return to the **Customize your footer** dialog. You should now see the **Contact Us** entry in the **List of Links**.

7. That's all there is to adding a link in the footer. Let's now add the **Privacy Policy** link. Can you handle it yourself? Sure, you can! Until it's time to enter the **Link Address**, that is. That's when you realize that you don't have a **Privacy Policy** page. So what gives? Don't worry. Simply enter **/privacypolicy.aspx** and create the link.

Now where did THIS address come from? I simply made it up. As you know, every web page has an address. The address is just a unique name you give to a web page so that your web server can send it down the wire when a viewer requests it. I just chose the first logical name that came to my mind. I could have called it `privacy.aspx`, `ljashdflkjhasdf.aspx`, or anything else I fancy as long as my website doesn't have another page with the same name.

The page doesn't have to exist when you create the link. But whenever you create the page (in Chapter 5, actually!), you'll have to call it `privacypolicy.aspx`, otherwise, the link won't work.

8. Go down to the **Footer Text** box and type your copyright notice. I'll type **© 2009, Acxede Corporation** for my website. You can enter whatever makes your lawyer happy.

Where's the © key? Nowhere. But you can type symbols such as ©, ®, and ™ with the help of the *ALT* key on your keyboard. To type the © symbol, hold down the *ALT* key and then type 0169 on the numeric key pad. Release the *ALT* key only after you've typed all four digits of 0169. As soon as you do, the © symbol appears. Note that this trick works only if use the numeric key pad; it won't work with the horizontal row of numeric keys above the first row of letters on your keyboard. The combination for the ® symbol is 0174 while the ™ requires 0153. Notebook computers don't have numeric keypads. If that's your predicament, the solution is to type the symbol in a word processor document or the Windows Character Map utility, cut it, and paste it in the **Footer Text** box. Visit this book's companion site at `http://officeliveguide.com/HowtoTypeCommonSymbols.aspx` if you need help on using either alternative.

9. Just as you did with the **Site Title** and **Site Slogan**, choose a font face and font size. And remember to stay away from the **B**, **I**, and **U** buttons.

10. At the very bottom of the **Customize your footer** dialog, there are three alignment options: **Left**, **Center**, and **Right**. Select **Center**.

11. Your **Customize your footer** dialog should now look like this:

12. Save your work and preview the website.

13. Click the **Contact Us** link in the footer. The **Contact Us** page should come up in your browser.

If you get a **Page Not Found** error, it could be because of two reasons:

- ❑   You probably forgot to enter the forward slash in the link address. Go back to the **Customize your footer** dialog, select the **Contact Us** link under list of links, and click the **Update** button. The **Link Properties** dialog opens. Add the forward slash at the beginning of the link address, save your work, and preview the site again.

- ❑   Your web server is configured a bit differently. If that's the case, you'll see `http:///contactus.aspx` in your browser's address bar instead of `http://yourdomainname/contactus.aspx`. To fix the problem, go back to the **Link Properties** dialog and specify the complete web address of the page in the link address. My link address will look like `http://officeliveguide.com/ contactus.aspx`, for example.

14. Note that the **Contact Us** page has the same header and footer as the **Home** page. Click the **Privacy Policy** link in the footer. Your browser should complain that it can't find the page. That's expected because you haven't created the page yet.

15. Close the preview window and return to **Site Designer**.

What just happened?

You set up the contents of your website's footer. I'll admit that it's not exactly pretty; there's ample scope to improve its look and feel. But Office Live Small Business doesn't have the necessary tools built in. So, we'll resort to some trickery, but not until Chapter 8.

Have a go hero – experiment with the footers

As was the case with the **Site Title** and the **Site Slogan**, try your hand at various options for customizing the footer until you're happy with the way the footer looks. Make sure that the links and the copyright notice don't look too big or too small. You might want to try adjusting the font size or changing the font face.

If your browser is Internet Explorer, try viewing your site in another browser such as Firefox or Opera. Font faces and font sizes that look absolutely fabulous in your favorite browser often look ugly in others. Therefore, it's a good idea to check your work in other browsers or even on other operating systems before you proceed.

Try changing the order of the links in the footer. I won't tell you explicitly how to go about it but here's a hint: open the **Customize your footer** dialog and look at the buttons on it.

Summary

In this chapter, you started building a template for the pages on your website. You decided upon a title for your site and, hopefully, a slogan as well. Then, you added a copyright message and a couple of links to the footer.

To recap:

- Your website's title should ideally reflect your business name or brand name.
- It's a good idea to come up with a slogan for your website. If you can't, then try substituting it with a short description of your business.
- A good title and a good slogan make your site 'findable'.
- Contact information and copyright notice are good candidates for the footer, so is a link to your privacy policy.
- You should test your site in multiple browsers and on multiple computers. You'll be amazed to see that what looks good on one, looks absolutely horrible in another. While that's hardly your fault, you're still responsible for choosing the right combination of font faces and font sizes that always look good.

In the next chapter, you'll build upon the work you've already done and add design elements that will make your site prettier.

3

Setting Design Options

Coming up with an attractive design for a website is not easy! If you want the individual design elements to blend into a harmonious whole, you must choose colors, fonts, and images that complement each other. The trouble, though, is that not everyone has the artistic eye necessary to achieve that harmony. Thankfully, Office Live Small Business comes with pre-built color palettes, design layouts, styles, and design options that are preconfigured by professional graphic designers. You can use these design configurations to build a professional-looking website with just a few mouse clicks.

In this chapter, you'll:

- ◆ Choose a theme for your website
- ◆ Choose a layout for the design elements in page headers
- ◆ Decide where the navigation links will appear on your web pages
- ◆ Choose a color scheme for your website
- ◆ Choose a font for the text on all your web pages

Choosing a theme for your website

A website's theme sets its tone. It gives you some sense of what the site is about, even if you haven't read the text. When you see pictures of people in dark suits sitting before computer monitors, for example, you associate the website with some kind of a professional outfit. But if you see pictures of butterflies, playhouses, and bright color schemes, a children's organization of some sort comes to mind.

Office Live Small Business sets the tone of your website by displaying a picture in the site's header. The picture and its physical setting constitute a **Theme**. The **Site Designer** offers a large selection of themes that are good for projecting just about any kind of organization. Offer plumbing services? You're covered. Own a garage? No problem! No matter what kind of business you own, you're likely to find a theme that will set the right ambience for your website.

Now that you understand what a theme is, let's go and choose one for your website.

Time for action – choosing a theme

1. Sign in to your Office Live Small Business account, if you haven't done so already, and go to **Page Manager**.

2. Pull down the **Design Site** menu from the **Page Manager** toolbar and select **Design site**. **Site Designer** opens.

3. Click on the **Theme** button on the ribbon. A pull-down menu displays the choice of themes for several categories of businesses.

4. Click on the category that's closest to your business. A selection of pictures appears to the right. I've selected **Education** because my website is about my book, and **Education** is the closest category I can find in the list. A selection of pictures appears to the right, as shown in the following screenshot:

If you have little or no design experience, you'll find Office Live Small Business's themes a Godsend. But if you are Photoshop-savvy, you might find the built-in themes quite pedestrian. If that's the case, don't fret! You can build a theme of your own. If you look carefully, **Custom Theme Image** is the first option in the **Themes** menu. But I am not going to discuss that option until Chapter 8. For now, just follow along by selecting a theme that best suits your website. Doing so will help you get a clear perspective of how themes work, which in turn, will enable you to obtain the right kind of image if you choose to go with a custom theme.

Click on the picture that catches your fancy. The **Themes** menu closes and the picture that you selected appears in the header of the page in the **Site Designer**, as shown:

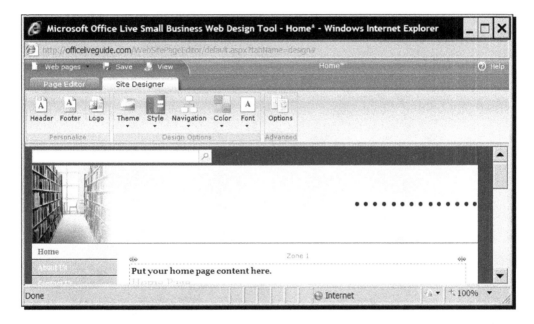

Well, that's nice! But where did the **Site Title** and **Site Slogan** go? Don't worry, they haven't vanished. What happened is that my theme has a light background. Because the title and slogan are white, you can't see them against the light background. Depending on which theme you choose, this may or may not happen to your headers. But if it does, rest assured, we'll fix it at the end of this chapter.

5. Save your work and preview the website.

6. Close the preview window and return to **Site Designer**.

What just happened?

You selected a theme for your site. A theme, in Office Live Small Business parlance, is just a picture that is displayed in the header area of your site. There's a wide variety of pictures and themes to choose from. And if you don't like any of them, you can upload one of your own. For now though, you have just selected one of the available ones.

Have a go hero – experiment with different themes

I recommend trying out all the available pictures in all the available categories before settling on a theme. Why? Because you might find the most suitable theme in a completely unrelated category. The **Automotive** category, for example, has a picture of wrenches. While it's quite appropriate for that category, it's also ideal for your website if you're a plumber. So go ahead, try every image available.

Choosing a style for your website

When you chose a theme, Office Live Small Business displayed the image of your choice in the page header. What if you don't like its location and want to move it around? You can do so by selecting a *style*. For example, here's my "bookshelves" theme laid out in a different style:

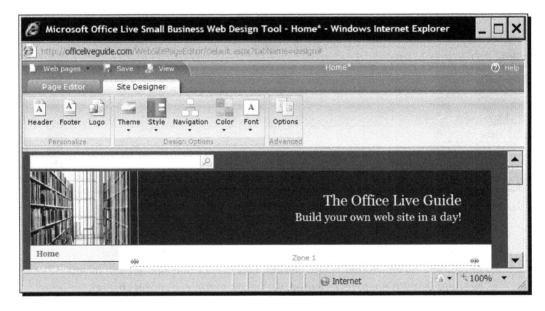

For every theme, Office Live Small Business gives you several styles to choose from. You don't have the option of positioning each element in the header individually, but the available styles move the image around, change its size, add special effects to it, and change the position of other header elements. There's a good chance that you'll like one of the available styles.

But what if you don't? In that case, you can always design a custom header. Designing custom headers is somewhat beyond the scope of this book. It needs a deeper knowledge of HTML, CSS, XML, and XSLT. But if you want to have a go at it anyway, you'll find the necessary instructions on this book's companion site at `http://www.officeliveguide.com/customheader.aspx`.

You don't have to go about it right now. It's a good idea to follow the rest of this book and build your website first. Once you're happy with the site in general, you can add bells and whistles such as a custom header. As a matter of fact, I'll give you several more suggestions as you work your way through this book.

Time for action – choosing a style

1. Click on the **Style** button on **Site Designer**'s ribbon. A pull-down menu displays the choice of styles.

2. Select the layout that you like. The **Themes** menu closes and you return to **Site Designer**. The page visible in **Site Designer** has the style that you just chose.

3. Save your work and preview the website.

4. Close the preview window and return to **Site Designer**.

What just happened?

You selected a style to go with your theme. As you can see, a style is just a layout for the header of your website. Each style positions the three header elements—Theme image, **Site Title**, and **Site Slogan**—differently. And some styles also alter the background of the header. The style that I just chose has a dark background. So, my **Site Title** and **Site Slogan** are visible again.

Have a go hero – experiment with different styles

As you did with the theme, it's a good idea to try out each of the available styles too. Who knows? You might find one that will bowl you over completely. Go ahead, give it a shot!

Choosing a navigation layout

The navigation layout determines where your website's navigation links appear. Office Live Small Business supports two kinds of navigation links: **primary links** and **secondary links**. Primary links lead to top-level pages or the main pages of your website's sections. Secondary links are subordinate to primary links. They lead to pages within a section.

The starter website you're working with is rather simple. You can think of it as having four sections: **Home**, **About Us**, **Contact Us**, and **Site Map**. Each section has only one page—its main page. Therefore, all the navigation links that you see on the left-hand side of your web pages are primary links, as shown:

Now, let's say that you just can't stop talking about your little outfit—you like to boast about your philosophy and your people. Naturally, you won't be able to fit everything that you've got to say on the **About Us** page that's already there. So, you decide to have a couple of subordinate pages: **Our Philosophy** and **Our People**. If you now bring up the **About Us** page in your browser, your site navigation will now look like this:

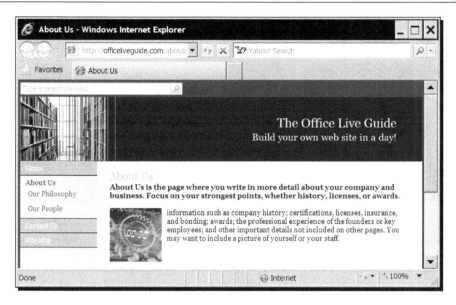

The new links, **Our Philosophy** and **Our People**, are secondary links.

Office Live Small Business offers three options for laying out the primary and secondary links:

- ◆ **Left**, which lays out both the primary and secondary links on the left-hand side of the page, just as in the previous screenshot.

- ◆ **Top & Left**, which lays out the primary links at the top of the page and secondary links on the left, like this:

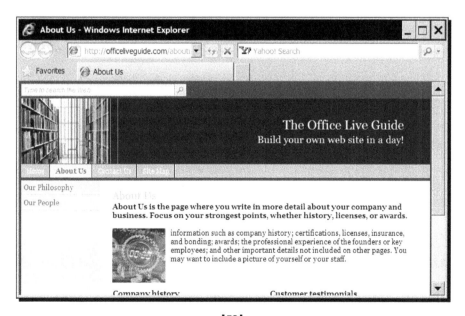

◆ **Top**, which lays out both the primary and secondary navigation links at the top of the page, like this:

So, let's choose the navigation layout for your site.

Time for action – choosing a style

1. Click on the **Navigation** button on the **Site Designer**'s ribbon. A pull-down menu displays the three possible navigation layouts.

2. Select **Top**. The **Navigation** menu closes and you return to **Site Designer**.

3. Save your work and preview the site.

4. Close the preview window and return to **Site Designer**.

What just happened?

You chose to display all the navigation links on your website at the top. When you preview the site, you can see that the four primary navigation links have moved to the top. You can't see any secondary navigation links yet, because your fledgling website has only four web pages, all of which represent primary navigation links. But when you add subordinate pages later on, you know where they'll appear in your website's navigation scheme.

Why did I decide, on your behalf, to display the navigation links at the top? Why not on the left? Or a combination of top and left? The reason will become clear when we set the site width in the next chapter. For now, just set it to **Top**.

Choosing a color scheme for your website

If you've ever visited the paint store with the intention of choosing a color for a single room in your house, you'll know how impossibly hard the task is! The task of choosing colors for a website is even harder by several orders of magnitude because you have to choose an entire color palette. Office Live Small Business spares you the pain and suffering by providing you with several built-in color schemes.

Time for action – choosing a color scheme

1. Click on the **Color** button on **Site Designer**'s ribbon. A pull-down menu displays the available built-in color schemes.

 At the bottom, you'll also see an option for creating a custom color scheme. But as usual, we'll leave that option for a later time.

2. Select the scheme that you like. The **Color** menu closes and you return to **Site Designer**. The page visible in **Site Designer** now displays the color scheme that you just chose.

3. Save your work and preview the website.

4. Close the preview window and return to **Site Designer**.

What just happened?

You selected a color scheme for your site. As a side-note, many people end up choosing counter-intuitive color schemes. Don't make that mistake with your site. Own a landscaping business? Choose a green-based color scheme. Run a daycare? A bright color scheme is more appropriate than a pastel one. While these choices sound like no-brainers, you'll be surprised how many people don't think of them.

Have a go hero – experiment with different color schemes

By now, you know the drill. Try out each of the available color schemes. Choosing color schemes is hard, even when experts build them for you. You'll often find that you like a color scheme except for one tiny application of it, to the navigation links, for example, which looks simply too gaudy. So, you might have to apply and reapply color schemes until you can make up your mind.

Remember, you can always customize any of the color schemes later. So, if you can't settle on the perfect scheme, choose one that comes closest to the scheme of your dreams. I'll show you how to customize it in Chapter 8.

Choosing a site font for your website

Site **Font** is the font that Office Live Small Business applies to all text on all of your web pages for which you don't explicitly specify a font. It's just like selecting a font for your word processing document. But keep in mind that elements such as the **Site Title** and the **Site Slogan**, which have their own font settings, as you saw in Chapter 2, are not affected by the site font; they retain their own font settings.

Pop quiz 3.1

1. **Georgia** and **Verdana** are the preferred fonts for websites because:

   A. They are narrow fonts. Therefore, you can squeeze in more text on a web page.

   B. They were designed especially for monitors. Therefore, they're easier to read on screen.

   C. They are the only two standards-compliant fonts.

Time for action – choosing the site font

1. Click on the **Font** button on the **Site Designer**'s ribbon. A pull-down menu displays seven font choices. These are the same seven fonts that you encountered in Chapter 2.

2. Select **Georgia** or **Verdana**. The **Font** menu closes and you return to **Site Designer**.

3. Save your work and preview the site. Notice that all pages now display the text in your chosen font.

4. Close the preview window and return to **Site Designer**.

What just happened?

You chose a font for all of the text on your website. When you add text to your web pages or edit what's already there, Office Live Small Business will display it in the site font.

Now, you might think that displaying all text on your website in a single font is a bit ham-handed. And you might be right. It's a good idea to choose a different font for headings and subheadings. So, what gives?

The site **Font** is really just the base font or the default font. If you want the headings and subheadings in a different font, you can select the text of the heading or subheading and change its font just as you would with a word processor.

Have a go hero – choose another font if you wish

I recommend **Georgia** or **Verdana** (see the answer to Pop quiz 3.1 if you can't remember why). But that doesn't mean that its the eleventh commandment. If you want to choose another font, for whatever reason, feel free to do so.

As a matter of fact, why not try out all the fonts to see which one you like the best?

Summary

In this chapter, you continued building your site template. You chose a **Theme**, a **Style**, a **Navigation** layout, a **Color** scheme, and the site **Font**. All these settings apply to your website as a whole, not only to individual pages. Therefore, all your pages look consistent.

Office Live Small Business offers built-in choices for most of these options. But if you're not really happy with the available choices, you can customize some of the options. You can customize a color scheme, for example, and build a custom theme.

At this stage though, I advise you to stick to the built-in options with a promise that I'll introduce you to the advanced options later on in the book. The reason is simple: at this stage, I just want you to get comfortable with **Site Designer** and take small steps towards building your site. You'll have ample opportunity later to tweak individual settings without losing any of the work that you've already done.

To recap:

♦ Your website's **Theme** is simply a picture that sets the tone for your site. Office Live Small Business has a large choice of themes built-in.

♦ A **Style** determines how the picture on the theme is laid out in your website's header. You can choose one of several available styles. You can't layout every element with pin-point precision individually, but the available styles cover a good number of possibilities.

♦ Your website can have two levels of navigation: primary and secondary. The **Navigation** layout determines where the primary and secondary navigation links will appear on your web pages. I advised you to choose the **Top** layout, which places both the primary and secondary links at the top of your web pages.

♦ A **Color** scheme determines the colors of individual elements on your web pages such as the page background and the color of navigation links. Office Live Small Business has a wide range of professionally designed color schemes built in.

♦ The site **Font** is the base font for the text on your web pages. But you can change the font of any block of text on any page, just as you would with a word processor.

In the next chapter, you'll give the finishing touches to your site template.

4

Setting Page Display Options

In the last couple of chapters, you customized the design settings such as site name, slogan, and footers that relate to your website's content. In this chapter, you'll customize settings that affect the look and feel of the pages on your site.

To begin this chapter, you'll:

- ◆ Choose a page width setting
- ◆ Choose a page alignment setting
- ◆ Choose a page background setting
- ◆ Get rid of the Office Live Small Business logo
- ◆ Get rid of the Windows Live Search box

At this stage, you'll have set all the site-level design options that you can possibly set using Office Live Small Business interactive dialogs. If you wish to customize your site even further, you certainly can, but you'll have to go beyond the ease of interactive dialogs and venture into writing custom instructions. If you're cringing at the thought of writing custom instructions, relax! It's easier than it sounds. Besides, I'll tell you what instructions to write and where to write them later in this chapter. All you'll need to do is type them.

Now, Office Live Small Business caters to the needs of everybody—from a complete novice to a seasoned pro. But to keep the program simple and accessible to novices, **Site Designer** hides some of the **Advanced design features** right out of the box. You'll have to activate them explicitly if you want to use them.

In the final section of this chapter, you'll:

- ◆ Enable **Advanced design features**
- ◆ Override the page width setting with a setting of your own

So, let's get cracking!

Setting site options

In Chapter 3, I showed you how a theme can alter the look and feel of your website. Let me now introduce a few additional options for fine-tuning the look and feel.

Time for action – opening the Site options dialog

1. Sign in to your Office Live Small Business account, if you haven't done so already, and go to **Page Manager**.

2. Pull down the **Design Site** menu from the **Page Manager** toolbar and select, **Design site**. The **Site Designer** opens.

From now on, I'll spare you the repetition of these two steps. By now, you should know how to open **Site Designer**. So, I'll simply tell you to go to **Site Designer**.

Click on the **Options** button on the ribbon. The **Site options** dialog opens:

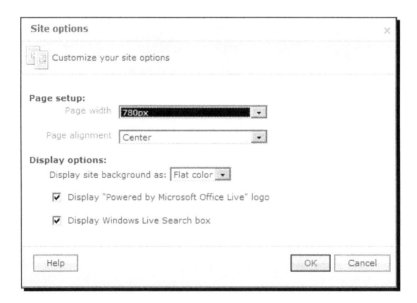

3. In the **Page width** dropdown box, select **780px**. This sets your web pages to be 780 pixels wide. The other width option is 100%, but I don't recommend it.

Why 780 pixels? Why not 100%?

Web pages that have a width of 100% adjust automatically to the resolution of a visitor's monitor. They allow you, the designer, to make the best possible use of available screen real estate. If you're designing an information portal, for example, you'll want to squeeze out every square inch of space that you can find, and then some; so, setting the page width to 100% is a no-brainer.

But small-business websites tend to be rather light on content. If you don't have much content and still set the page width to 100%, your web pages end up having just a couple of lines of text at the top and vast empty regions underneath. When that happens, you're tempted to fill those empty regions with irrelevant images, advertisements, animations, and other equally useless 'eye candy'. When you set the page width to 780 pixels, those empty areas don't appear as overpowering, and your site looks more balanced.

But there's also a disadvantage in choosing the 780px setting. It became popular when 800 X 600 was the most common monitor resolution. A 780 pixels wide web page filled the entire screen, after leaving 20 pixels for the browser's vertical scrollbar. But with advancing technology, people are gravitating towards bigger, wider, and higher resolution monitors. So, some people find the page width of 780 pixels too narrow.

And, I agree. I prefer a width of 980 pixels for small websites because it's neither too wide not too narrow. But as you can see, Office Live Small Business only gives you two choices: 100% or 780px.

Fortunately, there's a way to override the setting and make your web pages 980 pixels (or any number of pixels, for that matter) wide. I'll show you how to do that in the final section of this chapter. For now, just set it to 780px.

That said, if you're a budding writer, artist, or photographer, and have plenty of content for your web pages, you might find even 980 pixels to be too narrow. If that's the case, by all means set the page width to 100%.

4. In the **Page alignment** dropdown box, select **Center**. Note that you can choose this setting only if your page width is set to 780px.

Why not align the page to the left (or the right) margin?

Let's say your web page is 780 pixels wide and a visitor's monitor resolution is 1024 X 768 pixels. Even after you account for the 20 pixels that the browser's vertical scrollbar takes up, you're left with a band of blank space 224 pixels wide.

If you align your page to the left margin of the browser window, your pages will have the entire band of blank space on the right side of the page. When you center your page with respect to the browser window, you get a band 112 pixels wide on either side of your page. That gives a more balanced look to your page.

5. In the **Display site background as** dropdown, select either **Flat color** or **Gradient**.

Why not white?

When you set a fixed width, such as 780 pixels, for your website, it's a good idea to choose a colored background because it acts like a picture frame and focuses a vistor's attention on the content inside it.

Depending on the **Theme** and **Style** you choose, the background color may be light or dark. If the background is too dark for your liking, choose the **Gradient** option, which softens the bold background. If the background is light, **Flat color** is often the better choice.

However, I recommend that you try both the options and choose the one that you like the best.

6. Uncheck the **Display "Powered by Microsoft Office Live" logo** checkbox.

Why?

The logo that shows up at the bottom of your pages is an advertisement for Office Live Small Business. Just as you don't put up other people's advertisements in your office, there's no need to display them on your website. Besides, if you hover your mouse over the logo, you see a tooltip that invites you to **Get a free website and more** as shown:

You may not be paying a dime for your website, but you don't have to tell the whole world.

7. Deselect the **Display Windows Live Search box** checkbox.

Why hide the search box?

Office Live Small Business's search box is for searching the entire Web, not the contents of your website.

Although you'll often see such boxes on amateur websites, they aren't really appropriate for a business website, such as yours. After all, the reason that you're building your website is that you want to tell visitors about your business, not because you want to encourage them to search the Web.

Browse through any corporate website, including Microsoft's own, and you'll be hard-pressed to find a Windows Live or a Google search box. The reason is obvious: these boxes make sense only on search portals.

8. Save your work and preview the website. Confirm that the search box at the top and the Office Live Small Business logo at the bottom are now hidden.

9. Close the preview window and return to the **Site Designer**.

What just happened?

You just set the page and display options for your web pages. We're almost done with the site design part. Starting with the next chapter, we'll start building individual web pages. Then, we'll come back and tweak the site design setting in Chapter 8. But, let's lay down the groundwork for those tweaks in the next section.

Have a go hero – experiment with different page options

Although I handed down the edicts on the settings that you should choose, I recommend trying out alternate settings as well—as always. For example, you could try setting the background to Blank. Depending on your style and theme, a white background might look better, who knows!

Introducing Advanced design features

You've now set, or at least seen, every design option that you can set interactively. But what if you wanted to tweak some of the settings a little more? Make the font size of the footer links smaller, perhaps? Or change the width of the site to 980 pixels as we discussed?

Office Live Small Business does allow you to poke under its hood to change these and other settings. However, you must know some of those three and four-letter technologies to boldly go where no casual Office Live Small Business user has gone before! Because most casual users don't want to be bothered with HTML, CSS, XML, and XSLT (whatever they might mean), Office Live Small Business doesn't expose the features for overriding its settings right out of the box. You must explicitly enable Office Live Small Business's **Advanced design features**, which allow you to peek under the hood.

Time for action – activating Advanced design features

1. Sign in to your Office Live Small Business account, if you haven't done so already, and go to **Page Manager**.

2. Click on the **Site actions** tile to pull down the **Site actions** menu and then choose **Activate advanced design features** as shown.

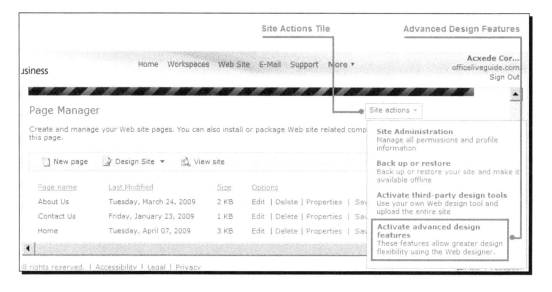

3. A confirmation dialog pops up as shown in the next screenshot:

4. Click **OK**. The dialog disappears and **Page Manager** refreshes. The **Advanced design features** are now enabled. Notice the first signs of change in the **Page Manager**—you should now see a new **Save as template** link against the entry for each page. Although you won't be doing anything with that link as yet, you'll soon see that it's a handy tool that will enable you to bring the same look and feel to all the web pages on your site. Notice the **Save as template** links in the next image:

What just happened?

You just enabled the **Advanced design features** that enable you to manipulate the inner workings of your website manually. Once you activate these features, Office Live Small Business adds several links and buttons to your site management dashboard. To see a complete list of changes to your dashboard, visit `http://www.officeliveguide.com/advanceddesignfeatures.aspx`.

By the way, you can deactivate these features by pulling down the **Site actions** menu again and selecting **Deactivate advanced design features**. But then you'll lose all the tweaks you made using the features. As you now are an advanced user anyway, we'll always leave them on.

Have a go hero – preview your site's stylesheet

Go to **Site Designer**. Can you spot an obvious change to its ribbon? It now sports a brand new button, **Style sheet**. Click it. The **Style sheet** dialog opens. At the top of the dialog is a blue link that says **View default CSS**. CSS stands for **Cascading StyleSheet**. A CSS defines how colors, fonts, positioning, and other layout elements apply to your web pages.

Click on the link. You'll see some code in the window that pops up. The code is, in fact, the CSS for your site. It determines how your site looks, trust me! But don't worry; you don't have to understand it. Just be aware of its function and that you can now manipulate it to your heart's content, thanks to the **Advanced design features**.

When you're done, close the window and then click the **Cancel** button in the **Style sheet** dialog to return to **Page Manager**.

Pop quiz 4.1

1. Your website's **Advanced Design Features** enable you to:

   A. Set your website's title

   B. Tweak design features not exposed in the **Site Designer** or the **Page Editor**

   C. Search the web using Windows Live Search

   D. Secure your website against unauthorized access

Using Advanced design features

Let me now give you a glimpse of the power that **Advanced Design Features** give you in styling your site. Let's change the width of your site from 780 pixels to 980 pixels.

Time for action – overriding the site width setting

1. Go to **Site Designer** and click on the **Style sheet** button on its ribbon. The **Style sheet** dialog opens as shown:

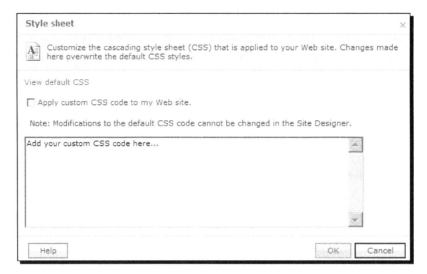

2. Select the **Apply custom CSS code to my Website** checkbox. Then, click inside the textbox that says **Add your custom CSS code here...**.

3. Delete the text in the box and type

   ```
   .MS_MasterFrame { width:980px; }
   ```

   as shown in the following screenshot:

Always type the CSS code EXACTLY as shown in the last screenshot. If you miss a semi-colon here or a colon there, the code won't do what it's supposed to do.

4. Click **OK**. The stylesheet dialog goes away and you return to **Page Manager**. Notice that the page in **Site Designer** is now wider.

5. Save your work and preview the website. Confirm that the page now appears wider.

If the page doesn't appear any wider, go back and check whether you typed the CSS code EXACTLY as shown, including the semi-colon, the colon, the curly braces, and the blank space between words.

6. Close the preview window.

What just happened?

You just added a style to your stylesheet that caused it to make your web pages wider. The stylesheet is just one of the features that you can access by activating the **Advanced design features**, but we'll use it extensively to alter the look and feel of your web pages in Chapter 8.

Summary

In this chapter, you gave finishing touches to your site template. You set the width and alignment for your web pages. Then, you chose a page background. Finally, you got rid of the Microsoft Office Small Business logo and the Windows Live Search box from your site template.

This completed the interactive design options available to you. Then, I showed you how to activate **Advanced design features** so that you can tweak some of the settings that you made interactively. As an example, I showed you how to override the site width setting with custom CSS.

To recap:

◆ You can let your web pages stretch to the width of the entire browser window or limit their width to 780 pixels. If your website is a typical small-business website, you are not likely to have lots of text content on your web pages. Therefore, web pages 780 pixels wide are likely to look better on your site than pages that take up the entire width of the browser.

◆ Pages that don't take up the entire width of the browser look better when they're centered in the window.

◆ You can choose a white or a colored background for your web pages. Colored backgrounds can be flat or they can have a gradient. You should choose a colored background, flat or with a gradient, because the backgrounds help.

◆ You can embed the Office Live Small Business logo in the footers of your web pages. I recommend that you hide it.

◆ You can also display a Windows Live Search box on your web pages. I recommend hiding it for two reasons. First, small websites—the kind you build with Office Live Small Business—tend to have only a few pages and therefore, don't really need a search box. Second, your site is not a search engine. Few people, if any at all, will come to your site to submit a search query to the Windows Live search engine.

◆ If your design requirements go beyond the options that you can set interactively, you can write custom instructions. To do so, you must enable Office Live Small Business's **Advanced Design Features**.

You have not finished yet, but the basic framework of your website is now in place. We'll come back and tweak a few more settings in Chapter 8.

In the next chapter, you'll finally start building and editing web pages.

5

Building Your Website's Skeleton

*In Chapter 1, I introduced Office Live Small Business's two main design tools, **Site Designer** and **Page Editor**. Then, in Chapters 2, 3, and 4, I showed you how to use **Site Designer** to customize your website's design options. In this chapter, I'll show you how to use **Page Editor** to create, edit, and delete web pages.*

The goal is to create a skeleton for your website by building four skeletal web pages that will serve as your website's foundation. In the theory of web design, there's no such thing as a skeletal web page. For the purpose of this discussion, I just made the term up to refer to web pages that every small-business website, including yours, should have at the bare minimum:

- A **Home** page that acts as the gateway to your site
- An **About Us** page that tells a visitor about you and your business
- A **Contact Us** page that enables visitors to contact you
- A **Privacy Policy** page that tells visitors how you use their personal information, such as their names and e-mail addresses

Come to think of it, the starter website that Office Live Small Business built for you already has the first three pages in this list. And for good reason, even the professional designers at Microsoft, who built the starter website, think that pages along these lines are pretty much essential for most small-business websites.

So, here's the plan:

- You'll begin by customizing the layout of the homepage. Once you're happy with the layout, you'll save it as a template that you can use to build new web pages. You'll then use this template to re-create the About Us and Contact Us pages. Why? Because you want all the pages on your website to look similar. The only way to do that reliably is to use the same template for all of them.

- Web pages need content. As I don't know much about your business, I can't provide you with readymade content for your web pages. But I'll give you tips on where to find good copy and pictures. I'll also give a few pointers on how to write good copy, if necessary. Using your new credentials as a copy writer, you'll write a copy for the two web pages that you've already built.

- You'll then add a new page, the **Privacy Policy** page, to your website. It goes without saying that you'll write a copy for that as well.

- Finally, you'll learn how to delete a web page by getting rid of the **Site Map** page.

By the time you're done with this chapter, you'll have a fully functional four-page mini-website—content and all. In the rest of this book, you'll build on this foundation by improving the content of these pages and adding supplementary pages that describe your products, services, or whatever it is that you sell or hype.

Editing the home page

The **Page Editor** is the tool for editing web pages in Office Live Small Business. Because I introduced the tool way back in Chapter 1, let's recap its features by opening the **Home** page.

Time for action – opening the Home page in Page Editor

1. Sign in to your Office Live Small Business account, if you haven't done so already, and go to **Page Manager**.

2. Click the **Edit** link under the **Options** column for the **Home** page. The page opens in Office Live Small Business **Page Editor**, as shown in the next screenshot:

 From now on, I won't repeat these instructions; when I want you to open a page for editing, I'll simply say, *Open such-and-such page in the* **Page Editor**.

What just happened?

You opened the **Home** page in the **Page Editor**.

Just like the **Site Designer**, the **Page Editor** too, has a Microsoft Office 2007-style ribbon at the top. The first two groups on the ribbon, **Font** and **Paragraph**, display familiar text editing commands. You can use these commands to format the text on the page just as you would on a word processor. If you want to underline a chunk of text, for example, select the text with your mouse and click the **U** button in the **Font** group on the ribbon, as shown:

To undo something you've just changed, press *CTRL+Z*.

If you want to right-justify a paragraph of text, place the cursor anywhere in the paragraph and click the **Align Right** button in the **Paragraph** group, as shown:

See? Just like a word processor, as I said.

The next group on the ribbon; **Insert**, displays commands that allow you to insert objects such as images, tables, and hyperlinks on the web page. Place the cursor anywhere in a zone—one of the regions on the page that's enclosed by red dotted lines, and click the **Horizontal line** button in the **Insert** group. Recall from Chapter 1 that a zone is an editable area on the page. All content on a page must reside within a zone. The **Horizontal line** button is shown in the next screenshot:

A horizontal line appears just below the cursor.

 CTRL+Z works not only with text, but also with any other object that you insert on a page.

The last group on the ribbon, **Advanced**, displays commands for manipulating some of the page's properties. Click on the **Page Properties** button, for example, and the **Page properties** dialog that you saw in Chapter 1 pops up.

It's quite convenient to be able to access the **Page properties** dialog from the **Page Editor**, as you just did, and also from the **Page Manager**, as you did in Chapter 1. You'll see that Office Live Small Business duplicates many such links to make your life easier.

Some buttons, such as the **Layout** button in the **Advanced** group, have a little downward-pointing arrow at the bottom. Clicking them will open a drop-down selection menu. Go ahead, try it!

Some other buttons, such as the **Navigation** button in the **Advanced** group, pop up dialog boxes where you can set properties.

The rest, such as the **Horizontal line** button, work on the web page's text as you just saw.

Don't worry if you don't understand what every command does at this stage; you'll go over them as you work along.

Have a go hero – experiment with Page Editor commands

Have a go at **Page Editor**'s commands. It wouldn't harm to click a few of them and get an idea of **Page Editor**'s features and capabilities. Add a table. Change the color of the text. Make the font bigger. Do whatever you please. And don't hesitate to experiment for fear of destroying the page. You can undo any change by pressing *CTRL+Z*.

How many changes can you undo?

I haven't really counted, so I can't give you an exact figure such as 23 or 127. But just as on a word processor, you can undo a series of changes with successive *CTRL+Zs*.

I've noticed, however, that on some pages, *CTRL+Z* works only once for no apparent reason. In any case, you can effectively cancel all unsaved changes to a web page by not saving the page.

How? Read on.

Just as in **Site Designer**, you can preview your website after modifying a page in **Page Editor**. Click the **View** button at the top of the ribbon. A dialog pops up enquiring whether you wish to save the changes. If you do, you'd click **OK**. But because you were just playing around with the page, you can click **Cancel** this time. As you'd expect, you'd click the **Save** button, right next to the **View** button, if you wanted to save your changes.

Close the preview window if it's still open, and return to **Page Editor**.

Choosing a page layout

Presently, the **Home** page is laid out with three content zones: **Zone 1** at the top, spanning the entire width of the page, and **Zone 2** and **Zone 3** below it, side-by-side. This is not the only layout available; **Page Editor** has several more. Some have three zones, others have two, and the rest only have a single zone. You can change the layout of a page at any time; even after you've built the page. Let's change the layout of the **Home** page.

Time for action – changing the Layout

1. Open the **Home** page in **Page Editor**.

2. Click the **Layout** button in the **Advanced** group of the ribbon. A menu drops down to reveal the available layouts as shown:

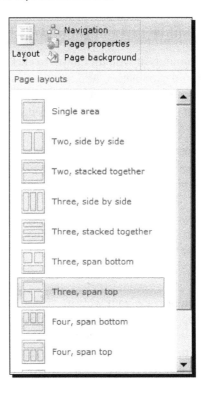

Notice that each option has a little thumbnail schematic of the layout that it represents. The option that corresponds to the present layout of your **Home** page, **Three, span top**, is highlighted.

3. Choose the **Three, side by side** option. The drop-down goes away and your **Home** page rearranges itself to conform to the new layout as shown:

4. Notice that although the **Page Editor** has rearranged the zones, it has preserved the content inside each.

But what if the layout I choose has fewer than three or more than three zones?

Aha! That gets the **Page Editor** into a fix. While transferring the content of three zones to three new zones is quite straightforward, there's no logical way of transferring the content of three zones to two or four zones. So the **Page Editor** takes its best guess in rearranging the content. If you don't like it, you can always cut some content from one zone and paste it into another.

5. Save the page and preview the website.

6. Close the preview window and return to the **Page Editor**.

What just happened?

You learnt how to change the layout of a page in **Page Editor**. So what's the big deal? Well, it's a good idea to use the same layout on most of the pages on your website, if not all. A common layout makes life easier for you as well as the people who visit your site—you can build your site faster, and visitors can find things on your pages in predictable places. Therefore, choosing a single good layout for your website often plays a prominent role in its success.

But then, you might ask, how come the good folks at Microsoft applied a different layout to every page on the starter site? The answer is that a single layout makes sense for small websites, such as yours, but sites with thousands of pages are often arranged into several logical sections and it's not unreasonable for pages in different sections to have different layouts. The starter site simply shows you an assortment of layouts, to give you an idea of how they look.

You'll use the **Three, side by side** layout you just chose. But you won't be adding content to each of the zones; you'll use the middle zone for content and the zones on either side for padding.

If multiple zones are available, why not use them?

In Chapter 4, I recommended that you set your site's width to 780 pixels because small websites often don't have much content when they start out. The same reasoning applies to the number of zones on your pages. More often than not, your content will fit comfortably in a single zone. If you choose a multiple-zone layout, you'll be hard pressed to find content to put into each of them.

And remember, even if you're using a single zone, two more are available, if need be, in the layout that you just chose. In fact, I'll show you how to use another zone without compromising the look and feel of your website when we get around to enhancing the **Contact Us** page in Chapter 7.

Customizing the page layout

That's better. Your page now has precisely the number of zones that you wanted it to have. But what if you don't like how *wide* a specific zone is? Fear not! You can change the width of any zone on your page quite easily.

Time for action – customizing a layout

1. Select the content in **Zone 1** and delete it.

> Unless you've played with the page layout and somehow managed to change the original order of the zones, the zones should be numbered 1, 2, and 3 from left to right. That's what I assume in the instructions. If your arrangement is different, read the instructions accordingly.

2. Select the content in **Zone 3** and delete it.

3. Just above the top corners of each zone, you'll see a pair of **drag handles** as shown:

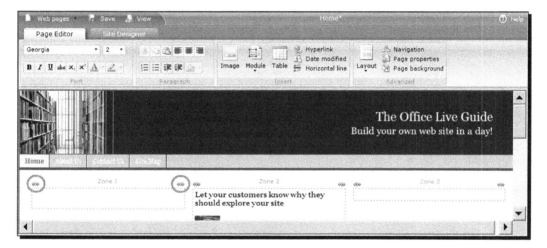

You can use them to adjust the width of the zone, just as you can use the drag handles on a word processor to adjust the width of the editable area of a document.

4. Click on the right drag handle of **Zone 1** and drag it towards the left. That should make **Zone 1** narrower.

5. Click the left drag handle of **Zone 3** and drag it towards the right. That should make **Zone 3** narrower.

6. Then use the drag handles of **Zone 2**, the middle zone, to stretch it on both sides. The end result should look something like this:

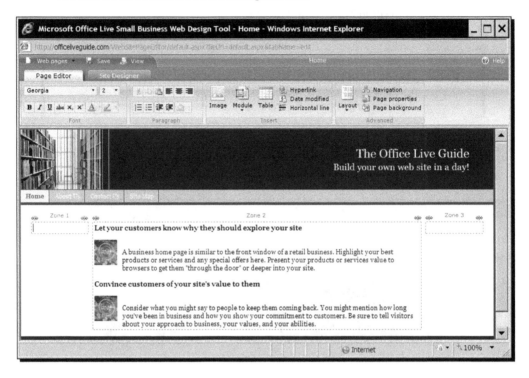

7. Select the content in **Zone 2** and delete it.

8. At this stage, the cursor should be positioned in **Zone 2**. If it isn't, click in **Zone 2** to place the cursor in it.

9. Type **Page Header**.

Notice that the text appears in the font that you set to be the site font in Chapter 3. The font also appears as selected in the font selector on the ribbon. Anything you type in any of the zones will inherit this font by default, unless you change it explicitly. In the following images, you'll see the text in **Georgia** because that's the font I set for my site. You'll see it in the font that you selected.

10. Select the text and increase its font size to **5 (18 pt)** using the font size selector on the ribbon.

11. Place the cursor just after the text that you just typed and click on the **Horizontal line** button on the ribbon. A horizontal line appears below the header text. Your page should now look something like this:

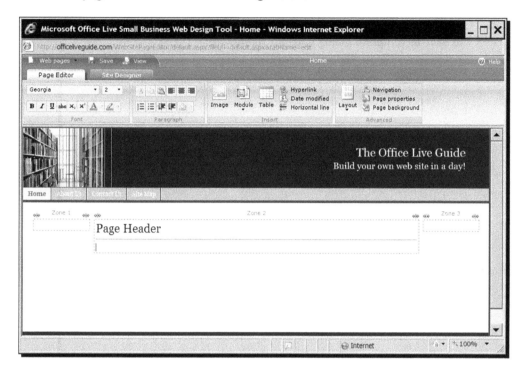

12. Save your work and preview the site.

13. Close the preview window and return to the **Page Editor**.

What just happened?

You learnt how to customize the layout that you've chosen for your web pages. From now on, you'll use this customized layout for all of your web pages.

Creating a template for future use

But how do you copy the layout to other pages? Simple. You create a template from this web page that you can use as the starting point for new web pages.

Time for action – creating and saving a page template

1. Go to **Page Manager**.

2. Click the **Save as template** link under the **Options** column for the **Home** page. The **Save as template** dialog pops up, as shown:

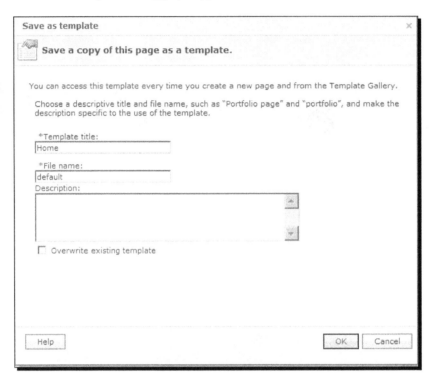

3. Change the **Template title** to **Base Template**.

4. Change the **File name** to **base**.

5. Type this **Description**: This is the site's base template. It has three columns side-by-side.

6. Click **OK**. The dialog goes away and you return to **Page Manager**.

7. Click the **Template Gallery** link in **Page Manager**'s left navigation pane to go to the **Template Gallery**.

8. The template that you just created appears in the list of templates in the gallery as shown in the following screenshot:

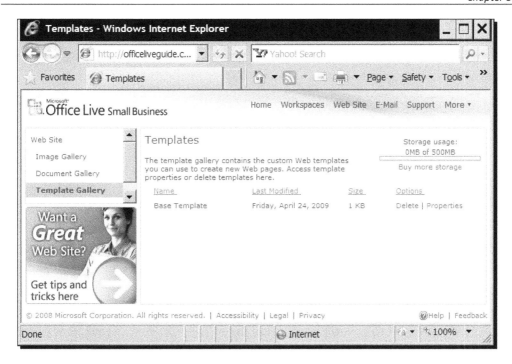

What just happened?

You created a template from your customized page layout. Office Live Small Business stored this template in a special area called the **Template Gallery**. You'll use this template as a starting point for all of the pages on your site. In fact, you'll build your first few pages using this template later in this chapter.

Have a go hero – view template properties

Just as the **Page Manager** helps you to manage web pages on your site, the **Template Gallery** helps you to manage your page templates.

Notice the familiar **Options** column with action links. Go ahead and view the properties of your only template. If you're up to it, you can delete the template and create it again.

What happens if I delete a template AFTER I use it to create a web page?

Don't worry, nothing bad happens. When you create a web page from a template, as you'll do very soon, Office Live Small Business copies the design elements from the template to the new page. So, even if you delete the template after creating a web page from it, that web page will remain hale and hearty.

At this stage, most people want to view their spanking new template. Unfortunately, there's no way to do so. You can only create templates and delete them. You can't edit them. The only way to "edit" a template is to create a page using that template, make the necessary edits, and save it as a new template.

 If you end up doing something like this, and want to save the edited template with the same name as the original, just select the **Overwrite existing template** checkbox in the **Save as template** dialog.

Creating content for the home page

The home page is important to you because you perceive it as a way to introduce your business to a visitor. But to be brutally honest, a visitor isn't interested in reading a long mission statement or how your grandfather founded the business during the Great Depression. He wants to find something quickly.

What are the dimensions of that bookcase that you sell? How long does it take to get the delivery? How does the 'thingamajig' that you make compare to the equivalent 'whatchamacallit' your competitor makes? How can he get in touch with you? Do you have a toll-free number? That's the kind of information that a visitor seeks when he arrives at your homepage.

 Content is still king!

Okay, repeat after me: the purpose of a website is to provide the information that a visitor seeks quickly, efficiently, and intuitively.

Although good looks don't hurt, how a site looks doesn't really matter. What matters is the content that it provides and how easily a visitor can find it. No matter what anyone tells you, *content is still king*.

And yet, many site owners frustrate visitors by providing gobbledygook such as this, instead:

Our mission is to quickly engineer technologically superior products utilizing our unique high-quality intellectual capital while promoting personal employee growth and continuing to continually facilitate progressive allocation of capital to cutting-edge research which enables us to cut the time-to-market (TTM) of our groundbreaking new products by approximately half that of the industry average.

If they can't think of such profound nonsense, they resort to adorning their homepages with pictures of pretty women seated before a computer and talking on the phone, or of guys in pin-striped suits carrying briefcases against a backdrop of tall glass buildings. Such pictures only make sense on your homepage if you sell computers, phones, suits, briefcases, or, even tall glass buildings.

The moral of the story is that, contrary to your first instincts, a web page shouldn't be a place for stuffing pompous text or meaningless eye-candy. It should be a place that helps a visitor find what he's looking for, quickly and intuitively.

So, what should you include on your homepage? Here's an example: the site I'm building with you is about this book. This is what I'll have on the home page:

Welcome small-business owners!

This website is the companion site to my book, Microsoft Office Live Small Business: Build and Customize your Business Website, published by Packt Publishing. The book will help you to build a website for your small business with Microsoft Office Live Small Business.

No, it won't morph you into a web-designer overnight, but it will show you how to squeeze the most out of Office Live Small Business to build an attractive, intuitive, and easy-to-use website without spending a penny.

Don't own it yet?

❑ Find out what Office Live Small Business is

❑ Learn more about the book

❑ View the table of contents

❑ Read a sample chapter

❑ Buy it from your favorite bookseller

Already a proud owner?

❑ View the errata

❑ Submit an errata

❑ Contact me

Each bulletpoint will ultimately become a hyperlink and lead to an information page on the topic it represents. And we'll add some eye-candy too. But for now, let's concentrate on the text.

My copy above consists of a brief statement of what the site is about, followed by information, which the two primary groups of visitors; prospective buyers and owners, are likely to want to know.

Have a go hero – write copy for your home page

Okay, it's time to try your hand at writing copy.

- Write a short paragraph about your business. Remember, no long history or bombastic mission statements; just a simple statement of what you do.

- Group the potential visitors to your site into two or three major groups, just as I did for my site. Then, list out bullet points that describe the information that they're likely to look for.

Do you have marketing materials for your business?

Do you use brochures, advertisement copy, one-page write-ups, or other similar marketing aids to promote your business offline? If so, you can use them as the starting point for your copy.

The copy doesn't have to be perfect; you'll have plenty of opportunities later to improve it. Like Rome, websites aren't built in a day either.

Use Notepad or a plain text editor for writing your copy. After you write the copy, you'll cut and paste it onto your Home page in the **Page Editor**. Recall that **Page Editor** acts as a word processor of sorts. Its styles may not necessarily be compatible with the styles of another word processor, such as Microsoft Word. Therefore, if you cut text from Microsoft Word and paste it on to **Page Editor**, its styles will overwrite the styles that you've set in **Page Editor**.

So, you should write your copy in a plain text editor, such as Notepad, which doesn't apply styles to text.

Building the Home page

Now that you have some copy for your **Home** page, let's go ahead and build it.

Time for action – add copy to the Home page

1. Open the document that contains the text that you've just written. Select the entire copy and copy it to the clipboard.

2. Open your **Home** page in the **Page Editor**.

3. Select the text **Page Header** along with the horizontal line below it and delete it; you don't really need a page header on the **Home** page.

4. Position the cursor in **Zone 2** and paste the text from your clipboard.

5. Format the text using **Page Editor**'s editing features. When you have finished, your page should look something like this:

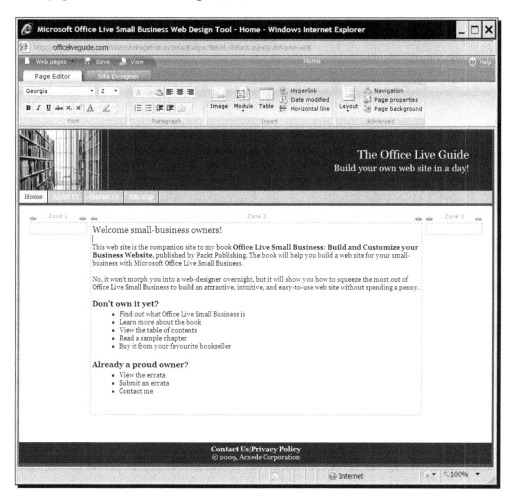

6. Save your work and preview the site.

What just happened?

You took the first stab at your **Home** page. Nothing exotic yet, but hopefully, you now have some meaningful content in place on the **Home** page. In the next chapter, we'll turn those bullet points into hyperlinks.

Re-creating the About Us page

Okay, your **Home** page is now all set. Let's move on to the **About Us** page. Yes, I know: Office Live Small Business has already created an **About Us** page for your starter website. The trouble is, it doesn't use the same template as your **Home** page.

Now that's a big no-no. Remember, we agreed that all web pages on your site will use your template. So, we'll have to find a way to apply your template to the **About Us** page.

Unfortunately, none exists. Once you create a web page, it's married to its template; in the present version of Office Live Small Business, at least. Your only option is to create it again using a new template.

Time for action – creating a new page from a template

1. Go to **Page Manager**.

2. Click the **New Page** link or icon on the toolbar. The **Create web page** dialog pops up as shown.

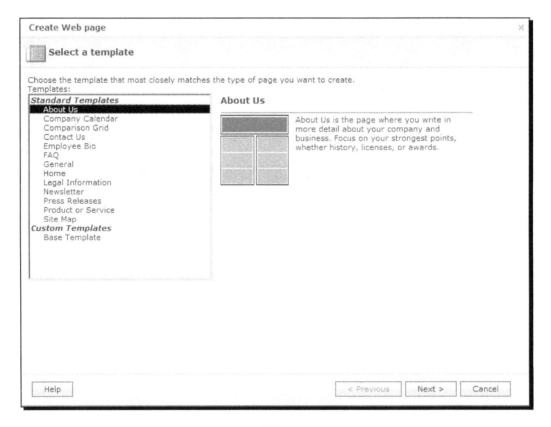

3. The first step in creating a web page is to choose a template for it. The **Create web page** dialog lists **Standard Templates**, which come bundled with Office Live Small Business, and **Custom Templates**, which you build yourself. Notice that the template that you built on earlier, **Base Template**, appears as a custom template in the selection box on the left. Select **Base Template** and click **Next**. The dialog asks you to **Choose page properties**.

4. Enter **About Us** as the **Page title**. This title appears in the title bar of the browser when you view it.

> The title **About Us** is appropriate when referring to companies, groups, organizations, or businesses that involve several people. If you're a magician, for example, and your website touts your services for children's birthday parties, then you may want to change the title to *About Me*, or *About Steve, the Magician* (assuming you're Steve, of course). It sounds a little less pretentious.
>
> For my website, I'm going to change the title to *About the Author*, which is more appropriate for a website that's dedicated to a book.

5. Type **aboutus** in the web address text box.

   The web address of the page will now be **aboutus.aspx**.

   It's a good idea to match a page's title and its web address. Because my page title is **About the Author**, I'll enter **abouttheauthor** in this text box. If your page title is **About Steve the Magician**, you should enter **aboutstevethemagician** here.

6. Select the **Overwrite existing page** checkbox.

   You're creating a new **About Us** page. But a page by that name already exists. By selecting this checkbox, you're telling Office Live Small Business to go ahead and overwrite it.

7. Select the **Show this page in the navigation bar** checkbox.

8. Notice that Office Live Small Business automatically enters **About Us** (or About Steve the Magician, or whatever you entered as the page's title) in the **Navigation title** text box.

9. Click **Finish**.

10. The **Create web page** dialog goes away and the **About Us** page you just created appears in the **Page Editor** as shown:

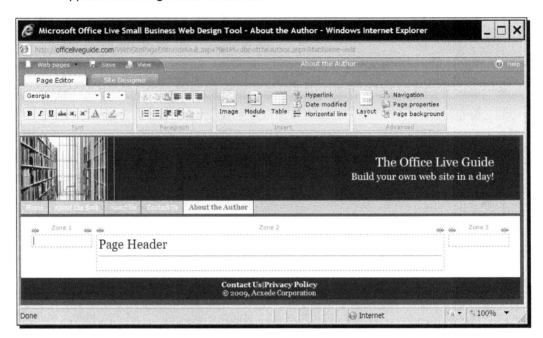

Hey! How come this picture shows both About Us and About the Author?

Elementary, my dear Watson! Because I didn't call my page **aboutus.aspx**. Had I done so, Office Live Small Business would have replaced the original `aboutus.aspx` with my new `aboutus.aspx`.

Because I called it `abouttheauthor.aspx`, the original **aboutus.aspx** is still intact. If you're in the same boat as I am in, you'll have to delete the **About Us** page. I'll show you how to do that later in this chapter.

11. Select the text **Page Header** in **Zone 2**, and overwrite it with **About Us** (or About Steve the Magician, or whatever).

12. Save your work and preview the page.

13. Close the preview window and return to **Page Editor**.

What just happened?

You replaced the **About Us** page that Office live Small Business automatically created for you with a new page that uses your custom page template. As we discussed earlier, it's a good idea to use a common template for all of the pages on your website. Hence this exercise.

Have a go hero – write copy for your about us page

The **About Us** page is for introducing your business to visitors. Do it concisely; nobody really has the time to read a five page profile. Here's the copy that I'm using for my website:

About the Author:

Rahul Pitre has been writing software of one sort or another for twenty-five years, the last dozen or so of which he has spent developing mostly websites and web applications. He runs Acxede, a software consulting and training firm in New York, where he oversees web application and content development for a variety of clients. He holds a Masters degree in Business Administration and Computer Information Systems.

Okay, it's your turn. Here's a rule of thumb that'll serve you well as you write some copy for this page:

Write about what people will want to know about you; not what you want to tell people about yourself.

Don't know where to start? Here are some points you might want to consider:

- ◆ What you do.
- ◆ How long you've been in business.
- ◆ The area that you serve.

  I highly recommend including your area and ZIP code in the copy. People often Google for phrases like *Magicians in NY 10701*. If you mention your general area and ZIP code in your text, there's a better chance of people finding you through search engines.

- ◆ Are you an authorized dealer for some big company?

  Again, people often search for phrases such as *authorized Sony service center NY 10701*.

- ◆ Have you received awards or citations for excellence?

- ◆ Are you a member of the Better Business Bureau or the local merchants' association?

- ◆ If your services are professional in nature, do you have the necessary qualifications? Licenses? Registrations? Insurance requirements?

If you prefer writing conversational text, write it in short paragraphs. Alternatively, you can use a combination of text and bullet points. But, keep it short. And for heaven's sake, don't write a mission statement.

> Remember to write the text in a plain text editor such as Notepad; not in a word processor.

Re-creating the Contact Us page

Now let us now create the **Contact Us** page again using your site's template.

Time for action – re-creating the Contact Us page

1. Go to **Page Manager**.

2. Click the **New Page** link or icon on the toolbar. The **Create web page** dialog pops up.

3. Select **Base Template** and click **Next**. The dialog asks you to **Choose page properties**.

4. Enter **Contact Us** as the **Page title**. This title appears in the title bar of the browser when you view it.

5. Type **contactus** in the web address textbox.

6. Select the **Overwrite existing page** checkbox.

7. Select the **Show this page in the navigation bar** checkbox.

8. Click **Finish**.

9. The **Create web page** dialog goes away and the **Contact Us** page you just created appears in the **Page Editor**.

10. Select the text **Page Header** in **Zone 2**, and overwrite it with **Contact Us**.

11. Save your work and preview the page.

What just happened?

You replaced the **Contact Us** page that Office live Small Business automatically created for you with a new page that uses your custom page template.

The **Contact Us** page is kind of unique. You might have noticed that the page you just replaced had a form for visitors to contact you. Normally, you'd have to write a little program to process the information they provide. The program would extract the information from the form and e-mail it to you. Thankfully, Office Live Small Business has a built-in component that does the job admirably. All that you need to do is to set the e-mail address at which you wish to receive the e-mails.

Because you re-created the page, that form is now gone. But don't worry; you'll add it in Chapter 7. The reason why I'm deferring it for now is that you haven't worked your way through a few prerequisites yet.

Creating the Privacy Policy page

When you created your website's footer back in Chapter 2, you created a link to your website's "as yet non existent" privacy policy as shown:

Contact Us|Privacy Policy
© 2009, Acxede Corporation

Let's now create a page that states your privacy policy and activate the link to it in the footer.

Time for action – creating a new page from a template

1. Go to **Page Manager**.

2. Click the **New Page** link or icon on the toolbar. The **Create web page** dialog pops up.

3. Select **Base Template** under **Custom Templates** and click **Next**. The dialog asks you to **Choose page properties**.

4. Enter **Privacy Policy** as the **Page title**. This title appears in the title bar of the browser when you view it.

5. Recall that in Chapter 2, you configured the **Privacy Policy** link in the footer to point to a page named `privacypolicy.aspx`. For that link to work, you must call this page `privacypolicy.aspx`. Every web page built with Office Live Small Business automatically gets the extension `.aspx`. So, just enter **privacypolicy** in the **Web address** textbox.

I've seen `.htm` **or** `.html` **extensions. What's** `.aspx`**?**

Office Live Small Business runs on a web development platform called ASP.Net, which uses the `.aspx` extension by default.

6. Because this page will only be accessible from the link in the footer, you don't need to include it in the page navigation. So, uncheck the **Show this page in the Navigation bar** checkbox.

7. Click **Finish**.

8. The **Create web page** dialog goes away and the **Privacy Policy** page that you just created appears in the **Page Editor**, as shown in the next screenshot:

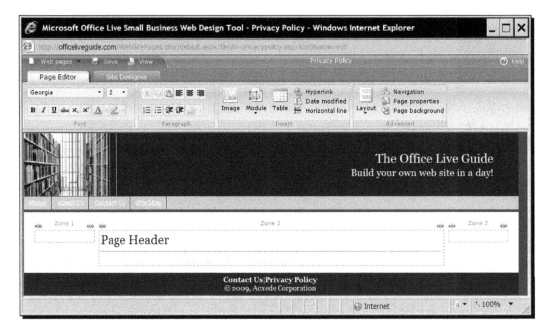

What just happened?

You created a brand new page for your website's privacy policy. You used the template that you built earlier in the chapter to create this page. Let's go ahead and write some copy for it.

Have a go hero – write copy for your Privacy Policy page

Your website will have a **Contact Us** page on which a visitor can provide his e-mail address and write you a short note as to what he wants. An e-mail address is considered personal information. So, it's a good idea to let people know what you plan to do with their e-mail addresses. You can declare your intentions in a **Privacy Policy** statement.

When you think of a **Privacy Policy**, a long document in verbose, understandable legalese with lots of *hereinunders* and *thereinafters* comes to mind. It doesn't have to be so. It's perfectly legal to make a legal document understandable. Here's the text that I'll use for my site:

> **OfficeLiveGuide.com's Privacy Policy:**
>
> The contact form on this website, should you choose to use it, sends the information that you enter, including your e-mail address, to me via e-mail.
>
> I use the information solely for responding to your message. I treat it with the strictest confidence and do not share or sell it.

Okay, it's your turn again. But before you start banging away at your keyboard, understand that your **Privacy Policy** is legally binding upon you. You must abide by what you say in it. If, like me, you declare that you won't use the e-mail address for anything other than replying to the person, then you can't use it to send a mass-mailing to him every month, for example.

A good way to generate the privacy policy is to use the Direct Marketing Association's Privacy Policy Generator at `http://www.dmaresponsibility.org/PPG`. You simply fill in an online questionnaire and the generator generates a custom **Privacy Policy** for you. You can then edit it to make it simpler and easier to understand.

 A **Privacy Policy** is a legal document. I'm not a lawyer and therefore not qualified to give you legal advice. Although DMA's Privacy Policy Generator is used widely, you should consult your lawyer in ascertaining the validity of the document that it generates.

As always, remember to write the text in a plain text editor such as Notepad; not in a word processor.

Building the Privacy Policy page

Once you are (and/or your lawyer is) happy with your copy, you can build the page.

Time for action – add copy to the Privacy Policy page

1. Open the document that contains the text of your **Privacy Policy**. Select all the text and copy it to the clipboard.

2. Open the **Privacy Policy** page in the **Page Editor**.

3. Select the text **Page Header** and replace it with **Privacy Policy**.

4. Position the cursor below the horizontal line under the header and paste the text from your clipboard.

5. Format the text using **Page Editor**'s editing features. When you have finished, your page should look something like this:

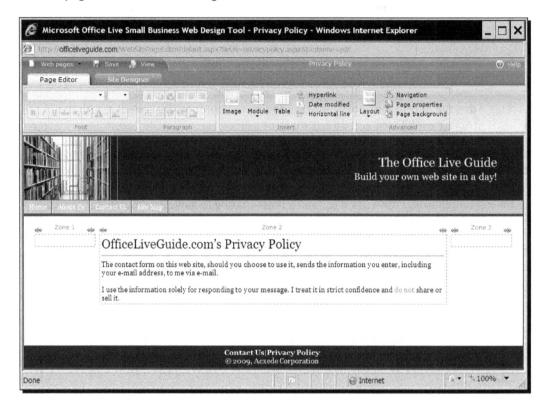

Feel free to format the text to your liking. For example, I added my domain name `OfficeLiveGuide.com` to the header and made the words "do not" red to draw attention to them. Just don't go berserk and make every word a different color.

6. Save your work and preview your site.

7. Click **Home** on the navigation bar to go to the **Home** page.

8. Click the **Privacy Policy** link in the footer. If you've done everything right, you should be looking at your **Privacy Policy** page.

What just happened?

You finished building your site's **Privacy Policy** page using either the copy you wrote for it, or the copy that the DMA's Privacy Policy Generator generated for you.

Deleting a page

You've come a long way! You now know how to edit existing web pages and create new ones. At some point, you'll invariably want to delete a web page, either because it's no longer necessary or because you messed it up so thoroughly that the only sensible option is to delete it! Let's prepare for that eventuality. To do so, you'll need a web page on your site that acts as a guinea pig. Let's volunteer the **Site Map** page.

What?!!! Don't we need a site map?

In a word: NO. Site maps exist for only one reason: to help visitors find a specific web page quickly. Although site maps are ubiquitous, they only make sense on large websites that house thousands upon thousands of pages. On such massive sites, just the site navigation can often not be detailed enough for a visitor to drill down to all major sections of the site.

 Your little website is likely to have just a few pages, each of which is accessible from the site navigation. So, the site map is merely a copy of your site navigation, and perhaps, an additional link or two such as the **Privacy Policy** link. In my opinion, it doesn't add any value to your website. I think it gives your site an aura of false grandiose. So, I recommend that you delete it.

But you might beg to differ, with all due respect, in which case you can simply read the instructions below, instead of executing them, and then come back to this section when you eventually need to delete some other web page.

Time for action – deleting a web page

1. Sign in to your Office Live Small Business account, if you haven't done so already, and go to **Page Manager**.

2. Click the **Delete** link under the **Options** column for the **Site Map** page.

3. The **Message form webpage** dialog pops up to confirm that you're within your senses to delete the page. Click **OK** to affirm that you are. Office Live Small Business deletes the page and the **Page Manager** refreshes to show the updated list of web pages on your site. Notice that the **Site Map** page no longer shows up in the list.

What just happened?

We decided that the **Site Map** page is somewhat redundant and deleted it. Into the bargain, you learnt how to delete web pages from your site.

How to delete a page—but only temporarily

From time to time, you'll want to get rid of web pages from your website, but only temporarily. Let's say, every year you run a promotion for Christmas and another for Valentine's Day. So, you build a "Promotions" page and put it up on your website in December. Come January, the page would have served its purpose and you would not want it on your site until February, that is, when your Valentine's Day promotion begins.

You can make a page go away from your site in two ways:

- ◆ Delete the page from your website
- ◆ Take it off the site navigation so that visitors can't access it

When you delete a page, you send it into oblivion; there's no way to get it back. When you take a page off the site navigation, on the other hand, you don't obliterate it; you just hide it from visitors. You can reinstate it if need be, simply by adding it back to the site navigation.

Naturally, taking the page off the site navigation appears to be the better option. But as it turns out, there's a catch—visitors may still be able to go to the page if they've bookmarked it. Besides, it may appear in search engine results for a few days even after you've removed it from site navigation.

The second option of deleting the page comes with its own obvious baggage: you can't quickly alter the Christmas promotion page and turn it into a Valentine's Day promotion page. You've got to start from scratch to build a new one.

You might think that you're caught between a rock and a hard place. But don't worry; there's an easy way out. If you need to get rid of a web page temporarily, you can save it as a template and then delete it. When you want to resurrect it in a new incarnation, you can use the template that you saved to build a new page quickly.

Summary

Congratulations! You have covered a lot of ground in this chapter. You transformed the cookie-cutter starter website into your own distinctive website. Lots more remains to be done, of course, but you have got off to a good start.

To recap:

◆ Your site's **Home** page is the gateway to your site. You should avoid the temptation to fill it up with nonsensical text and pictures.

◆ Good websites use a common template for their pages so that visitors can find what they're looking for in expected locations. Office Live Small Business makes it easy to build templates by giving you the ability to save any web page as a template.

◆ The success or failure of your site depends, to a great extent, on how easily and intuitively visitors can find what they're looking for. Therefore, you should write short, but meaningful copy. Remember, content is still king.

◆ Every website that collects personal information from visitors should have a privacy policy. Remember, a privacy policy statement is a legal document; so do what you say you'll do in the document. Also, you may want to consult your lawyer before you finalize your privacy policy.

◆ Although it's easy to delete web pages from your site permanently, there's no way to get rid of them temporarily. But you can work around the problem by saving the page as a template before deleting it and then recreating it from the template when you want it back.

In the next chapter, you'll build your site's information pages; pages that describe your products and services. If you're getting a bit restless about the pedestrian appearance of your site, have some patience. You'll embark upon a beautification drive of your site in the rest of the book, after you build the information pages in the next chapter.

6
Building the Information Pages

In Chapter 5, you built the skeleton of your website. The skeletal pages help a visitor get an overall sense of your business and help to create a positive image of the business in a visitor's mind.

But that's not the real reason that you're building a website. You're building it because you want people to know what you do, the products you sell, the services you provide, or simply your opinion, if you don't really sell anything.

The skeletal pages you've built so far don't seem to do any of that. Now, don't get me wrong! I'm not saying that those pages don't matter. They do. However, they're more like condiments: they just add flavor to the information that you really want to convey on your site.

In this chapter, you'll build the pages that display the information that your visitors are really looking for: pages that describe your products or services. I'll call them information pages to distinguish them from the utilitarian skeletal pages that you built in Chapter 5.

So, here's the plan:

- ◆ Decide the information that should go on the information pages
- ◆ Divide the information into logical sections
- ◆ Sub-divide the information in each section into logical topics
- ◆ Decide how to organize the sections and topics on the website
- ◆ Create web pages to fit the organizational scheme

By the time you're done with this chapter, your website will almost be complete information-wise. In the next couple of chapters, you'll learn how to improve the presentation and utility of the information using images, links, tables, and even some eye-candy.

Selecting and organizing information for your site's information pages

Information pages provide answers to questions that a visitor may have about the products and/or services your business offers. Naturally, they should contain information about your products and/or services.

This book's companion site: a case study

Because I don't know what kind of business you're in, I can't provide the exact information for the pages on your site and suggest how to organize them. But, I'll do the next best thing: I'll show you how I'd select and organize information for the information pages of this book's companion site—the site I'm building as you're building yours. By using my site as a case study, you'll easily be able to select and organize information for the information pages on your website.

Step 1: Decide the purpose of the website

The first step is to be clear about why I'm building this website. If I state the purpose of my site in clear terms, I'll be able to decide who my target audience is likely to be and what information they would want to seek on my site. Here's my site's statement of purpose:

I'm building my website because:

- ◆ I want to promote my book and make people aware of it.
- ◆ I want to provide information about my book to those who might be interested in building their own small-business websites with Office Live Small Business. The information I provide should help a visitor to decide whether the book is right for him/her.
- ◆ I want to provide additional information and support to the smart people who've already bought my book.

Step 2: Specify potential visitors and classify them into groups

For my site, the likely visitors are small-business owners who want to build their own website on a shoe-string. I can divide them into two major categories:

- ◆ Those who haven't bought my book yet
- ◆ Those who have bought my book

This classification is obviously based on the assumption that people who visit my site are either evaluating my book for a possible purchase, or have already bought it and are looking for additional information.

Surely, there are many other ways to classify the potential visitors to my site. But this classification makes the most sense because they align most closely with the purpose of my website. Although rival authors, friends and family, and random visitors are also potential categories of visitors, I won't consider them because their interests don't align with the website's purpose.

Step 3: Wear the visitors' hats and think of questions they'd ask

Visitors from each of the two groups will ask a different set of questions. The best way to speculate on what they'd want to know is to put myself in their shoes and make a list of questions they would ask. Here's my list:

Questions that people who haven't bought my book yet might ask:

- Hmm! This appears to be the website for a book. What's this book about?
- What the heck is Office Live Small Business?
- Can I build a personal website with Office Live Small Business?
- What exactly is in the book?
- Can I download sample chapters?
- I'm a beginner (or an advanced user). Is this book written for my level? Can it really help me to build my own website?
- Do I need any fancy computer equipment?
- Is building a website really this easy?
- What do other people have to say about this book?
- Where can I buy this book?

Questions that people who have already bought my book might ask:

- Are there links to the online references mentioned in the book, so that I don't have to type in long web addresses?
- Are errata available online?
- Can I download the e-book if I've already bought a copy?
- I found a typo or an error in the book. Can I submit an erratum?
- Is there any bonus content or supplementary material?
- I have a question for the author. Is there an easy way to contact him?
- Office Live Small Business is not for me. Can I get my money back?

Of course, this list is not exhaustive. I don't have to think of every possible question anyone might ever ask. As long as I cover the most common questions, I'll do just fine. Besides, building a website is an ongoing process. I can always add or delete content later, based on how visitors use the site.

Also, keep in mind that I haven't included every question that came to my mind in the list above, so as to keep this case study easy to follow. But if you visit the companion website at `http://www.officeliveguide.com`, you'll find the end result of this exercise remarkably similar to what I've presented here. So, I've followed what I've preached.

Step 4: Select questions that are worth answering

Just because someone might ask a question doesn't necessarily mean that I'd want to answer it. For example, someone who has bought the book might want to know whether he can get his money back.

Naturally, I'd like to think that not many would ask that question. But I wouldn't necessarily want to answer it even if someone actually did. That question is really not for me to answer; it should be addressed to the bookseller from whom the visitor bought the book. So, it doesn't exactly relate to the purpose of my website.

Some other questions in the list may not have answers. For example, it would take a while after the book is published for people to write reviews or express their opinions about it. So, I don't have an immediate answer to the question: *What do other people have to say about this book?*

So, the next step is to narrow down the list of questions and select only those questions that relate to your website's goals. Here's my shortened list:

Questions that people who haven't bought my book yet would ask:

- Hmm! This appears to be the website for a book. What's this book about?
- What the heck is Office Live Small Business?
- What exactly is in the book?
- I'm a beginner (or an advanced user). Is this book written for my level? Can it really help me build my own website?
- Do I need any fancy computer equipment?
- Where can I buy this book?

Questions that people who have already bought my book would ask:

- Are there links to the online references mentioned in the book, so that I don't have to type in long web addresses?
- Are errata available online?

- I found a typo or an error in the book. Can I submit an erratum?

- Is there any bonus content or supplementary material?

- I have a question for the author. Is there an easy way to contact him?

Step 5: Classify questions into topics

Answers to these questions will constitute the content of my site's information pages. But some of the questions might be related. Consider these two questions:

- Are online errata available?

  I found a typo or an error in the book. Can I submit an erratum?

They are both about the broader topic, *Errata*. Therefore, I can lump them together. In other words, I can translate the questions that I've selected into broad information topics. Here's my translated list:

Information for people who haven't bought my book yet:

- Hmm! This appears to be the website for a book. What's this book about?

  I'm a beginner (or an advanced user). Is this book written for my level?

  Can it really help me to build my own website?

  Do I need any fancy computer equipment?

  Translation: *Book Description*

- What the heck is Office Live Small Business?

  Translation: *About Office Live Small Business*

- What exactly is in the book?

  Translation: *Book contents*

- Where can I buy this book?

  Translation: *How to purchase*

Information for people who have already bought my book:

- Are there links to the online references mentioned in the book, so that I don't have to type in long web addresses?

  Translation: *References*

- Are errata available online?

  I found a typo or an error in the book. Can I submit an erratum?

  Translation: *Errata*

◆ Is there any bonus content or supplementary material?

Translation: *Online content*

◆ I have a question for the author. Is there an easy way to contact him?

Translation: *Contact information*

Each of the two groups of visitors; prospective buyers and current owners, will have a dedicated section on the website. Each section will then have a web page for every topic about which the visitors might ask questions.

Each section page on the website will be a top-level page. That means a link to it will appear on the site's primary navigation right next to the **Home**, **About Us**, and **Contact Us** links.

Each topic page in a section will be a second-level page on the website and a link to it will appear on the second-level navigation bar.

Step 6: Reword the section and topic names with phrases suitable for the website

The section and topic names that I've come up with are rather pedestrian. I had better replace them with something that sounds a little more professional. So, I'll reword them as follows:

About the Book

◆ Book description

◆ What's Office Live?

◆ Sample content

◆ Buy it

Owner's Section

◆ References

◆ Errata

◆ Online content

◆ Contact information

Step 7: Eliminate redundant information and finalize the page hierarchy

That's better! But before I finalize this information hierarchy, there's one more thing that I can do: eliminate redundant pages and arrange the topics logically.

The page for *About the Book* section and the page for *Book description* topic seem to have overlapping content. Why not consolidate it on the *About the book* section page? That way, I can eliminate an unnecessary topic page.

And the *Contact information* topic under the *Owner's Section* is also somewhat redundant because my website already has a **Contact Us** page. So, I'll get rid of that too.

Now, my streamlined information hierarchy looks like this:

About the Book

- ◆ What's Office Live?
- ◆ Sample content
- ◆ Buy it

Owner's Section

- ◆ Online content
- ◆ References
- ◆ Errata

A few more examples

You might ask: *What good is this example to me? I'm not building a companion website for your book.*

Well, even if your website is not about a book, the process of selecting and organizing the information for your site's information pages remains essentially the same. Let's hustle through a couple more examples in the following sections to prove the point.

A website for children's art classes

Let's say you run art classes for children. A fast track to your website's information page hierarchy might run something like this:

Purpose:

I'm building a website because:

- ◆ I want to inform parents of children (ages 5-12) about the drawing, painting, and pottery classes that I run
- ◆ I want to publish a list of classes currently in session
- ◆ I want to publish my registration policies and procedures

Types of visitors:

- ◆ People looking for after-school activities for their children; particularly, art classes
- ◆ People ready to register their children for classes

Questions:

Following are the questions that people who want to know more about the coaching classes would ask:

- What programs do you run?
- Who teaches the classes?
- Are the programs taught at different levels or do all children attend the same class?
- What will my child learn in the drawing (or painting, or pottery) class?
- How many weeks does a class run for?
- How much does it cost?
- Would you return my money if my child doesn't like the class?

People who are ready to register would ask the following questions:

- When does the next drawing (or painting, or pottery) class start?
- Is a spot available in the next drawing (or painting, or pottery) class?
- Do you have a schedule of upcoming classes?
- How can I register?
- When do I need to pay?
- Do you accept credit cards?

Final page hierarchy:

Our Programs

- Drawing
- Painting
- Pottery

Register

- Class schedule
- Registration
- Payment
- Policies

There's no single right way of arriving at the final page hierarchy. You may come up with a hierarchy different from mine. And a third person may think of yet another variation. But as long as the three of us start with the same statement of purpose, we will arrive at similar topics. We just may arrange them a bit differently.

A website for an appliance repair service

Let's take another example. Let's say, you run an appliance repair service. A fast track to your website's information page hierarchy might look something like this:

Purpose:

I'm building a website because:

- I want to inform people about my services
- I want to inform people about the kinds and brands of appliance I service
- I want to give people an idea of the rates I charge

Types of visitors:

- People who want to get their appliances serviced or repaired

Questions:

Following are the questions that people who want to get their appliances serviced would ask:

- Do you repair refrigerators (or stoves, or washers, or dryers, or whatever)?
- Do you perform routine preventive maintenance?
- Do you repair Maytag washers (or Kenmore fridges, or Bosch stoves, or whatever)?
- How much do you charge for a service call?
- Do you carry the necessary spare parts?
- Is your work guaranteed? For how long?
- Do you accept credit cards?
- Do you work in the evenings? On weekends?

Final page hierarchy:

Services

- Preventative maintenance
- Repairs
- Types and brands serviced
- Working hours
- Rates
- Payment methods
- Warranty

Here's an example of how two people may arrange the same information differently:

I came up with a page hierarchy for the appliance service site with the idea of keeping the site simple. But if you're a bit more adventurous, you might decide that the topics in my list actually belong to two broad categories: services and information about services. You might then come up with a page hierarchy as follows:

Services

Preventative Maintenance

Repairs

About Our Services

Types and brands serviced

Working hours

Rates

Payment methods

Warranty

In fact, this is a better page hierarchy. But that said, there's nothing drastically wrong with my original page hierarchy.

As I've stressed often, developing a website is an ongoing process. Some people will build their site my way. Some others will build it their way. And still others will initially build it my way so as to get up-and-running quickly and then change it gradually to their own hierarchy.

Have a go hero – selecting and organizing information for your website's information pages

By now, you should have a good handle on the process of selecting and organizing information. It's time to put your knowledge to good use.

Go ahead and do this exercise for your own website. Remember, I kept the questions simple for illustrative purposes. You don't have to. So, let the creative juices flow!

But here's a word of caution: don't be too ambitious and create a hierarchy of twenty sections and a hundred and fifty-seven topics. After all, you're building a website for your small business, not for General Electric.

Although I've grown hoarse saying it, I'll say it again: building a website is an iterative process. Start small and cover broad details in the first pass. Once you build a small but complete site, you can always expand it in the next iteration.

Creating section pages

Now that you're ready with your site's information hierarchy, let's go ahead and build the information pages. You'll create the section pages in this section and the topic pages in the next.

But I have the same problem in presenting a walk-through of creating a section page as I had with telling you how to select and organize information: I don't know anything about your website.

So, here's what I'll do. I'll present the walk-through using my website as an example. All you'll do is substitute my section name (**About the Book**) with yours. If you're building the appliance repair site we just talked about, for example, you'll substitute **About the Book**, with that site's section name, **Services**.

Time for action – creating a section page

1. Go to **Page Manager** and click the **New Page** button on its toolbar. The **Create Web page** wizard opens asking you to select a template.

2. Select **Base Template** under **Custom Templates**—that's the template that you created in Chapter 5 for your website. Click **Next**. The wizard asks you to choose page properties.

3. Type the name of the section you're creating this page for in the **Page title** text box. I'm creating this page for the **About the Book** section. So, I'll enter **About the Book**.

4. Type the web address for this page in the **Web address** textbox. Recall that the web address is a unique address for a web page that appears in a browser's address bar. I'll type **aboutthebook**.

5. Select the **Show this page in the Navigation bar** checkbox. Office Live Small Business automatically fills in **About the Book** in the **Navigation title** textbox. That's fine with me.

6. I want this page to be at the top level of navigation, which is where Office Live Small Business has automatically put it in the **Select parent** drop-down box. That's fine with me too. The **Choose page properties** page is shown as follows:

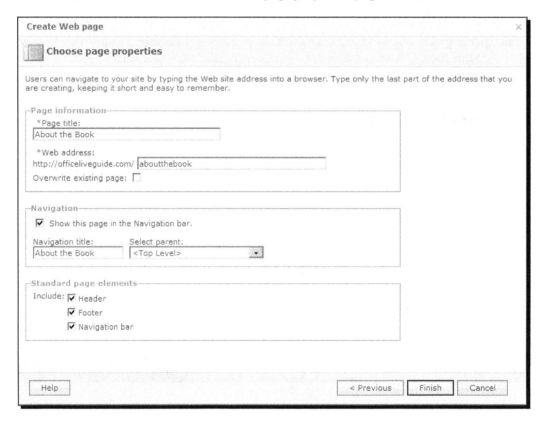

7. Click **Finish**.

8. Office Live Small Business creates the new page and opens it in **Page Editor** in a new window.

9. Save your work and preview the website. It should look something like this:

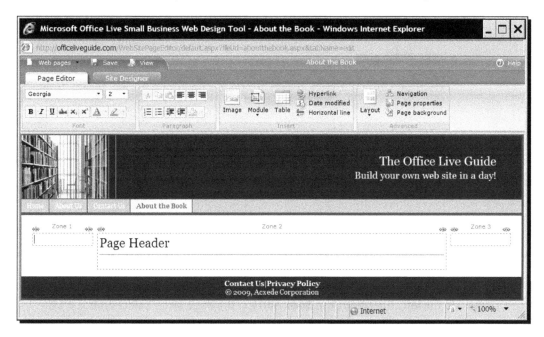

10. Notice that **About the Book** is now a new link on the site's main navigation bar. But there's a small problem. The new link is right at the end. I'd rather have it between **Home** and **About Us**. Let's fix that right away.

11. Close the preview window and return to **Page Editor**.

12. Click the **Page properties** button in the **Advanced** group of **Page Editor**'s ribbon. The **Choose page properties** dialog opens.

13. Click the **Edit navigation position** button in the dialog window. The page's **Navigation** dialog opens, as shown:

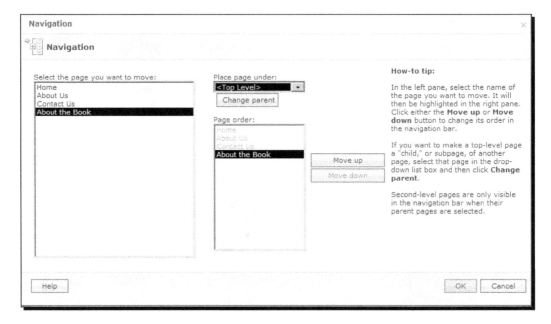

14. Click the **About the Book** entry in the **Select the page you want to move** selection box on the left. The **About the Book** entry in the **Page order** selection box on the right automatically gets highlighted.

15. Click the **Move up** button twice until the link is between **Home** and **About Us**. Click **OK**. The Navigation dialog closes.

16. Click **OK**. The **Choose page properties** dialog closes and you return to **Page Editor**.

17. Notice that the **About the Book** link in the navigation bar has moved to its intended location.

18. While you're there, select the words **Page Header** in **Zone 2** and overwrite them with **About the Book**.

19. Save your work and preview the site. It should now look something like this:

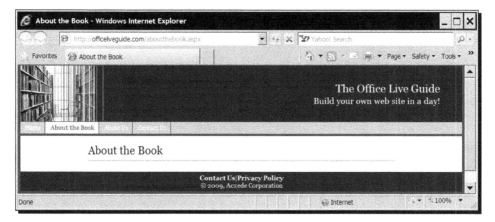

20. Close the preview window and return to **Page Editor**.

21. Close the **Page Editor** and return to **Page Manager**.

What just happened?

You just created your first information section page. As you can see, you didn't have to do anything different to create the page. You followed, essentially, the same steps you followed in creating the pages in Chapter 5.

The only thing that you did differently here was to move the page to a different location on the site's main navigation. In fact, you can change the location of absolutely any page that's on the navigation bar by following these exact steps.

Have a go hero – creating the rest of the section pages

If your information hierarchy has more than one section, you'll have to create a page for each of them. Go ahead and do so now. And remember to position the new pages appropriately on your site's main navigation bar.

Pop quiz 6.1

1. How many levels of navigation can a website build with Office Live Small Business have?

   A. One

   B. Two

   C. Three

   D. Four

Creating topic pages

All right, your section pages are now ready. But you're not done yet. You still need to add the topic pages. That's what you'll do in this section.

Just as I did with creating the section pages, I'll present the walk-through using my website as an example. I'll create the first topic page (**What's Office Live?**) under **About the Book** section. All you'll have to do to follow along is substitute **What's Office Live?** with the name of your topic.

Time for action – creating a topic page

1. Go to **Page Manager** and click the **New Page** button on its toolbar. The **Create Web page** wizard opens asking you to select a template.

2. Select **Base Template** under **Custom Templates**. That's the template you created in Chapter 5 for your website. Click **Next**. The wizard asks you to choose page properties.

3. Type the name of the section you're creating this page for in the **Page title** textbox. I'm creating this page for the **What's Office Live?** topic. So, I'll enter **What's Office Live?**

4. Type the web address for this page in the **Web address** textbox. I'll type **whatsofficelive**.

5. Select the **Show this page in the Navigation bar** checkbox. Office Live Small Business automatically fills in **What's Office Live?** in the **Navigation title** textbox. That's fine with me.

6. Office Live Small Business automatically places it at the top level in the **Select parent** selection box. That's not where I want it. I want it to go under the **About the Book** section. In other words, I want the **About the Book** page to be this page's parent. To make that happen, pull down the options in the **Select parent** selection box and select **About the Book**. (You'll select your section name, of course.)

7. Click **Finish**.

 Creating a new page is getting to be fairly routine. The process is the same, no matter what kind of page you're creating. So, from now on, I'll simply tell you to *create a new page* instead of repeating the steps above and save a few trees in the bargain.

8. Office Live Small Business creates the new page and opens it in **Page Editor** in a new window.

9. Edit the text of the page title in **Zone 2** to read **What's Office Live?**

10. Save your work and preview the website. It should look something like this:

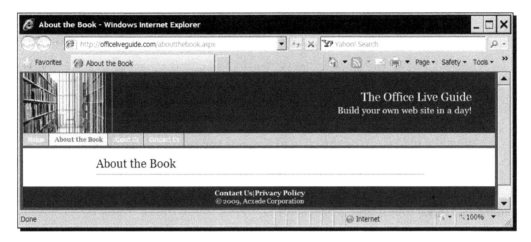

What just happened?

You created your first topic page. So, what's different about it? Well, it's not a top-level page. Notice that it's not on the site's main navigation bar. It's on a second navigation bar that has just appeared. Also, notice that the **About the Book** link on the main navigation bar is highlighted.

The net effect is that the topic page appears to be a subordinate to the section page, which is exactly what the intention was.

Click on the **About Us** link. The second-level navigation bar goes away. That's to be expected because it made sense only in the context of the **About the Book** section. It only appears when you click on the **About the Book** link on the main navigation bar.

Have a go hero – creating the rest of the topic pages

Go ahead! Create a page for each of the topics under each of your sections now.

Creating content for the section pages

People come to websites, including yours, to find information quickly. The role of the section pages is to lead them to the desired information quickly and intuitively.

Therefore, treat a section page like a table of contents for that section; it should basically contain a very brief description of the content of each of the topic pages, and underneath it, a link leading to that topic page.

Don't fill up section pages with long essays or marketing materials. The important information on your site is really going to be on the topic pages. Use the section pages to lead a visitor to the right topic page quickly.

Here's an example—possible content for the **About the Book** section page on my site:

> *Microsoft Office Live Small Business: Beginner's Guide* is a practical beginner's guide to planning and building a small-business website with Office Live Small Business in next to no time.
>
> Never heard of Office Live Small Business? Learn more.
>
> What's in the book? See the table of contents and read a sample chapter.
>
> Sold on the idea? Buy the book and build a website for your small business.

The underlined phrases are actually links that lead to the **What's Office Live?**, **Sample content**, *and* **Buy it** topic pages, respectively.

This text tells the visitors what the book is about, without wasting their time and leads them to the related topic pages. With such section pages, visitors can find the desired content quickly. Of course, you can write the same content in many different but equally effective ways. I've proposed a rule of thumb above, which won't let you down.

Have a go hero – writing content for section pages

Try your hand at writing content for each of your section pages. Don't worry; it doesn't have to be perfect. But make a serious attempt at writing something that's short and to the point. When your draft is ready, transfer the text to the corresponding section page on your website.

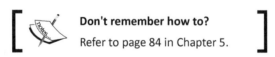

Don't remember how to?
Refer to page 84 in Chapter 5.

Creating content for the topic pages

The meat of your website's content will reside on the topic pages. But that doesn't mean you should write verbose essays on these pages. Provide detailed but to-the-point information.

Where do you start? Go back to the list of questions that prompted you to create this topic. Arrange those questions in a logical order. Then, write short answers for each of them.

Tips for writing content for topic pages:

◆ Write simple and short sentences. But don't overdo it. You don't want your text to read like a Dr. Seuss book.

◆ Prefer short paragraphs.

◆ Use bullet points instead of sentences wherever possible.

◆ Write in active voice.

◆ Use words that your audience would commonly use. Driving a car is the same thing as operating a vehicle but a lot easier to understand.

◆ Write grammatically correct sentences.

◆ Spell check your text.

Have a go hero – writing content for topic pages

Write content for each of your topic pages. Again, it doesn't have to be perfect. You'll have plenty of opportunities to revise the text later.

When your draft is ready, transfer the text to the appropriate topic page on your website.

Summary

In this chapter, you added information pages to your website. Your website is now structurally complete. You have all the necessary web pages in place. To recap:

◆ Information pages on your website provide answers to questions that visitors may have about your products and services.

◆ There is no standard way of arranging information pages on a website. Their structure and hierarchy depends on the specifics of your business. However, there's a more-or-less standard methodology that you can follow to come up with the structure and hierarchy of information pages for any website.

◆ Creating information pages with Office Live Small Business's tools is easy. You create them in the same way that you'd create any other web page: from a template.

◆ Office Live Small Business has a two-level navigation hierarchy. The section pages go at the top level and the topic pages go at the second level. The topic pages hold the meat of your site's content. The section pages help a visitor to arrive at the right topic page.

Your website now has all the text it needs. In the next chapter, you'll make your pages friendlier, prettier, and more useful by adding elements such as links, pictures, and tables.

7
Improving the Presentation

Web pages that merely display text are rather monotonous. Presentational aids such as pictures, tables, maps, slide shows, and hyperlinks help you present information in a more digestible format. But using these elements on web pages is somewhat of a mixed bag. Manipulating pictures or hyperlinks is relatively straightforward, but working with live maps or slideshows is not. Thankfully, Office Live Small Business includes tools that make working with these elements a snap.

In this chapter, you'll learn how to use these tools. Specifically, you'll learn how to:

◆ Use **Page Editor**'s modules, which really are drop-in components of sorts, to add features that normally require some programming

◆ Create hyperlinks

◆ Upload pictures and place them on your web pages

◆ Present data in a tabular format

By the time you work your way through this chapter, your web pages will stop looking like word processor documents and start looking like real web pages.

Introducing Page Editor's modules

In the early days of the Web, websites consisted mostly of static documents that displayed text and an occasional picture. But as the Web evolved, such static websites slowly gave way to dynamic web applications.

Web applications are like computer programs. They process data or information stored in databases of some sort and produce an output that you and I see as web pages.

Office Live Small Business is a web application too. It stores your information—site name, theme, color settings, text, images, and practically everything you create or set using **Page Manager**, **Site Designer**, and **Page Editor**, into a database. When a visitor requests a page on your site, Office Live Small Business does its magic and assembles all of these pieces of information into a web page and sends it to the visitor's browser.

But if a computer program is generating your web page, why not have it add a few advanced elements to the page? That's exactly what Office Live Small Business does. It includes little self-contained programs, called *modules*, which you can simply drop on your web pages to do fancy stuff that, otherwise, would require you to hire a programmer.

Setting up a contact form with the Contact Us module

Remember your **Contact Us** page had an e-mail form that disappeared when you re-created the page using your custom template? Let's roll up our sleeves and add it back using one of **Page Editor**'s modules.

Time for action – creating a contact form

1. Go to **Page Manager** and open the **Contact Us** page in **Page Editor**.

2. Place the cursor at the bottom of **Zone 2** and pull down the **Module** menu as shown:

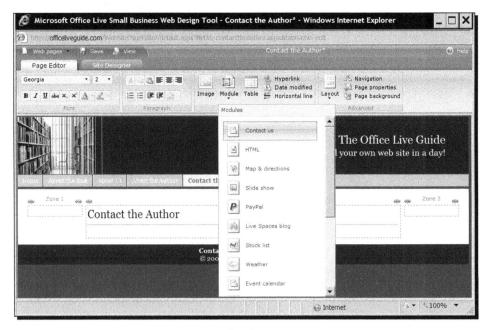

3. Click the **Contact Us** option. The **Change the Contact Us settings** dialog opens as shown in the next image:

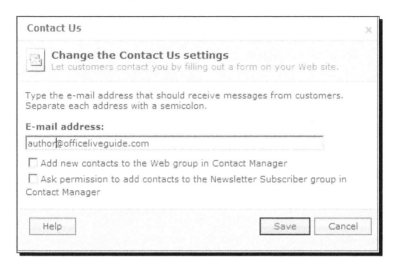

If this is the first time that you're looking at this dialog, you might see a yellow band asking you to activate the **Contact Manager**. It is a rudimentary **Customer Relationship Management** (**CRM**) application. Just click the link in the yellow band to activate it.

4. Enter your e-mail address in the **E-mail address** textbox, and deselect the two checkboxes underneath it.

Office Live Small Business's **Contact Manager** application is fairly decent. It allows you to capture e-mail addresses of people who contact you through your website's **Contact Us** page. But some people are interested in collecting e-mail addresses from **Contact Us** forms; others are not. For simplicity's sake, I'll assume that you fall into the latter group. But if you do want to collect e-mail addresses, feel free to select these checkboxes.

5. Click **Save**. The dialog goes away and an e-mail form appears on your **Contact Us** page.

6. Save and preview the page.

7. Fill in the form on the page and click **Submit**.

8. If all goes well, you should see a "thank you" page informing you that the message was sent.

9. Office Live Small Business packages the information that you entered into an e-mail message and sends it to the address that you just set. Go ahead, check your mailbox.

 If you don't see the message in your mailbox, you probably mistyped your e-mail address in the module's settings. Go back to the **Page Editor**, right-click on the module, and choose **Properties...**. The **Change the Contact Us settings** dialog opens, where you can correct your e-mail address.

10. Close the preview window and return to the **Contact us** page in **Page Editor**.

What just happened?

You used one of Office Live Small Business's built-in modules to create a contact form for your website.

As I mentioned earlier, you'd normally need program code, or script, to send out an e-mail message from a web page. Office Live Small Business has packaged the code within the **Contact Us** module. All you had to do was to drop the module on your page and choose a few relevant settings. In fact, the module does more than just send a message, it also validates the form and ensures that all of the required information, as indicated by the red stars on the form, is present on it before sending it out to you. If any of the required information is missing, Office Live Small Business displays a pop-up error message. Go ahead, try it!

By the way, you can change a module's settings and properties by right-clicking on it and choosing **Properties...** on the pop-up menu, which opens the properties dialog for the module.

Adding contact information

All right, people can now contact you through e-mail. But that's not the only contact information that people usually look for. Some might want to know your mailing address or the location of your office. Some others may simply want to call you or fax a document to you. Therefore, it's a good idea to include this information on your **Contact Us** page.

I run my business from home. What if I don't want to display my address on my website?

That's a fair question. You don't really have to display your address on your website if you work from home.

Perhaps, you don't need to display the contact information. Take the site I'm building, for example. While I certainly intend to answer questions that readers like you may have, I don't want people calling me at an inconvenient time just to ask a question about Office Live Small Business. Therefore, the contact form is, without question, the appropriate contact vehicle for my website.

If your situation is like mine, it's perfectly all right to have just the contact form on your **Contact Us** page. But for most businesses, a phone number, a fax number, a P.O Box, or anything besides just a contact form will help to convince people that you run a legitimate business and not some shady operation.

Time for action – adding contact information

1. Go to **Page Manager** and open the **Contact Us** page in **Page Editor**, if it's not already open.

2. Make **Zone 2** narrower by dragging its right drag-handle towards the left as shown in the next image:

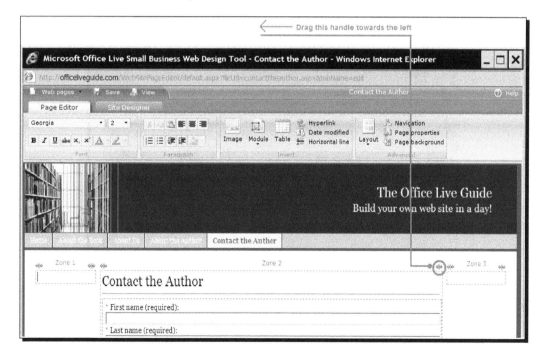

3. The page should now look like this in **Page Editor**:

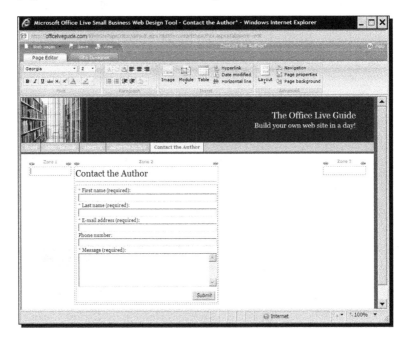

4. Now make **Zone 3** wider by dragging its left drag-handle towards the left. The page should look like this in **Page Editor**:

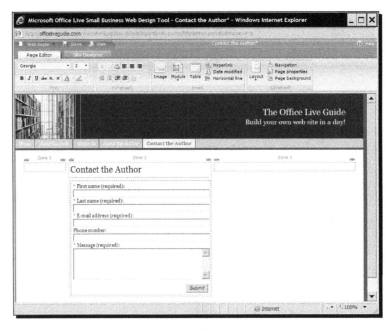

5. Now, type your address information in **Zone 3**.

6. Save your work and preview the page. It should look something like this:

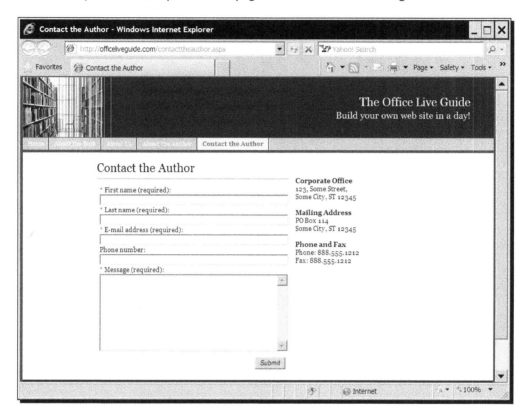

7. Depending on how wide your address lines are, your page might look a bit off-center, like the picture above. Let's fix that.

8. Close the preview window and return to **Page Editor**.

9. Drag the right drag-handle of **Zone 2** and the left drag-handle of **Zone 3** to the right until the page appears centered.

10. Save your work and preview the page. It should now look something like this:

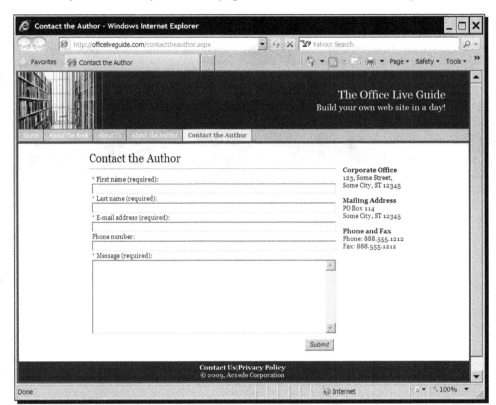

11. That's much better! There's roughly equal white space on either side of the content.

12. Close the preview window and return to **Page Editor**.

What just happened?

You added your contact information to the **Contact Us** page, so that people can contact you by phone, fax, or snail-mail as well.

In the bargain, you also learned how to adjust your page template to accommodate contents of different widths.

Displaying a map and driving directions

Now that people can get your address from your website, why not make their life easier by providing a map and driving directions? Sure, not a problem! **Page Editor** has a **Map and directions** module just for that purpose. Here's how it works:

You drop it on a page and fill in the address that you want a map of. The module gets the map from Microsoft's MapPoint service and displays it on your web page along with a hyperlink for directions. When you click on the hyperlink, MSN's Driving Directions page appears in a new window.

Time for action – creating a map and driving directions page

1. Go to **Page Manager** and click the **New Page** button on its toolbar. The **Create Web page** wizard opens, asking you to select a template.

2. Select **Base Template** under **Custom Templates** and click **Next**. The wizard asks you to **Choose page properties**.

3. Type **Map** in the **Page title** text box.

4. Type **map** in the **Web address** text box.

5. Leave the **Show this page in the Navigation bar** checkbox deselected.

6. Click **Finish**.

7. Office Live Small Business creates the new page and opens it in **Page Editor** in a new window.

8. Edit the text of the page title in **Zone 2** to read **Map**.

9. Save your work and preview the website. It should look something like this:

10. Close the preview window and return to **Page Editor**.

11. Place the cursor below the horizontal rule and pull down the **Module** menu from the ribbon.

12. Click on **Map & directions**. The **Map & Directions** dialog pops up. It has two tabs at the top: **Location** and **Display Options**. You're presently on the **Location** tab.

13. Select your country in the **Country or region** drop-down. Then type in the **Address** textbox.

14. Click on the **Display Options** tab.

15. Select the **Use an interactive map** checkbox.

16. Choose the **Large** radio button for the **Size** option.

17. Select the **Show driving directions** checkbox.

18. Select the **Show address** checkbox.

19. Click **OK**. The **Map & Directions** dialog closes. The page now displays a map of your neighborhood in **Page Editor**.

20. Save your work and preview the page. It should look something like this:

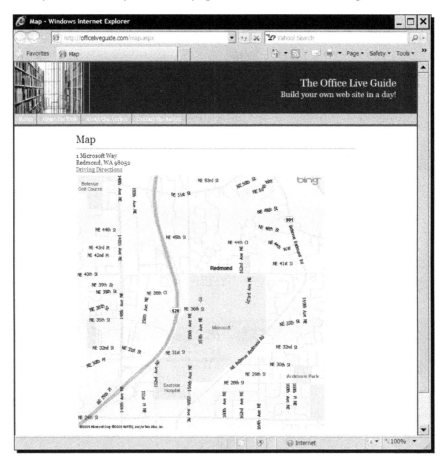

21. Notice that the map module displays your address and a hyperlink for driving directions.

22. Click the **Driving Directions** hyperlink. The Microsoft Live Search website's driving directions page pops up in a new window with your address as the **End** address. A visitor can now enter her address as the **Start** address and get driving directions to your office.

23. Close the preview window and return to **Page Editor**.

What just happened?

You used Office Live Small Business's **Map & directions** module to display a map of your neighborhood on your website. And you didn't have to write a single line of program code to do it. Now that you've worked with a few modules, you'll begin to appreciate their power.

Have a go hero: customize the Map & directions display

You can customize the look and feel of the map to an extent. Right-click on the **Map & directions** module on your page and select **Properties....** The **Map & directions** dialog that you just saw pops up again. Click on the **Display Options** tab. Now, try choosing a different combination of options. The module will customize the map display depending on the options you choose. Choose a combination that you like the best.

Trying out a couple of other modules

All of the modules that you see on the **Module** pull-down menu work more or less in the same fashion, only the settings differ from module to module. So, why not try out a couple of other modules? Let's give the **Weather** and the **Stock list** modules a try. Once you understand how modules work, you'll be able to use any of them with ease.

Time for action – trying out Weather and Stock modules

1. Go to **Page Manager** and create a new page. Call it the **Test** page.

 You'll use this page as a guinea pig to experiment with new features. Of course, it goes without saying that you'll delete it before taking your site live.

2. Add a **Weather** module to the **Test** page. The properties are quite straightforward:

 ❑ Enter a ZIP code and click **Search** to see a list of cities in that ZIP code

 ❑ Choose whether you want to show a four-day forecast; the default is one-day

 ❑ Choose a unit for displaying the temperature

3. Save your work and preview the page.

4. Close the preview window and return to **Page Editor**.

5. Add a horizontal line below the **Weather** module.

 Don't remember how to? See page 72.

6. Now, add a **Stock list** module to the **Test** page. It displays current prices for the stock symbols of your choice. Can you work with it by yourself? Good.

7. Save your work and preview the page.

8. When you have finished, close **Page Editor** and return to **Page Manager**.

Didn't I tell you that working with modules is a piece of cake? As we go about building your site, we'll use other modules as well. So, don't worry at this stage if you don't understand what some of them do.

What just happened?

You tried out two more modules: the **Weather** module and the **Stock list** module on the **Test** web page. The takeaway from this trial is that you work with all of Office Live Business's modules in essentially the same way. First, you drag-and-drop the module on your web page. Then, you right-click on it to bring up its properties dialog. Finally, you set the properties in the dialog.

Then, bam! Office Live Small Business does its magic behind-the-scenes and your page gets a slick new feature.

One of the advanced modules, the **List Publisher** module, gives you the ability to create a simple database and display the information in it on your web pages. A practical case that illustrates its use is beyond the scope of this book. But if you're interested, you can read a tutorial on it on this book's companion site at `www.officeliveguide.com/listpublishermodule.aspx`.

Creating hyperlinks

Earlier in the chapter, you created a page to display a map of your neighborhood on your site. The page looks quite nice. But the trouble is that there's no way to get to it unless you know its web address because it doesn't appear on either of the navigation menus. That's not really a desirable scheme of things. Wouldn't it be great if you could hyperlink to the Map page from the **Contact Us** page? That's precisely what you'll do next.

Time for action – creating a hyperlink to the Map page

1. Bring up the **Contact Us** page in **Page Editor**.

2. Add the words **Map and directions** just below your address in **Zone 3** as shown:

3. Select the words **Map and directions** with your mouse and then click the **Hyperlink** button in the **Insert** group on **Page Editor**'s ribbon. The **Insert a link** dialog pops up as shown:

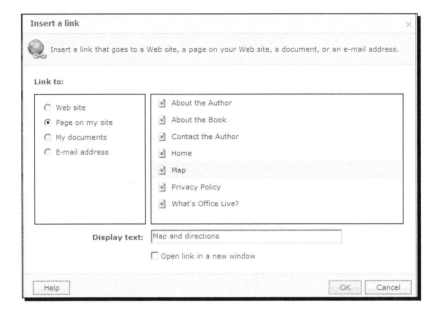

4. You want to link to another page on your own website. So, choose the **Page on my site** radio button in the box on the left. A list of all the pages on your site appears in the box on the right.

5. Click on **Map** in the list of pages. The entry gets highlighted.

6. Click **OK**. The **Insert a link** dialog closes and you return to **Page Editor**. Your new hyperlink now looks like this:

7. Save your work and preview the page. When it comes up in the preview window, click on the hyperlink. It should take you to the **Map** page.

8. Close the preview window and return to **Page Editor**.

What just happened?

With this simple step, you just learned how to create a website out of stand-alone web pages.

Although your hyperlink linked to a page right on your site, it's just as easy to link to just about any web page anywhere on the Internet. To connect to a page on another website, simply select the **Website** radio button in the **Insert a link** dialog. A textbox for entering the address of the page you wish to link to, will appear in the box on the right. Enter the address and click **OK**.

Have a go hero – working with hyperlinks

Bring up the **Test** page that you created earlier while working with modules. Create the following hyperlinks:

♦ A hyperlink that reads **Go to Google** and links to `http://www.google.com`

♦ A hyperlink that reads **E-mail me** and links to your e-mail address

    Hint: select the **E-mail address** radio button in the **Insert a link** dialog.

Don't hyperlink to e-mail addresses

Although you now know how to hyperlink to e-mail addresses, I don't recommend doing so on your website unless you want to receive tons of spam. Use the **Contact Us** module instead, when you want to provide a way for visitors to contact you.

Displaying pictures

Okay, you now know how to use modules and create hyperlinks. Let's now move on to pictures.

Although pictures appear on a web page, they don't really reside there; they're stored in a folder on your web server. A reference to the location of the picture resides on the web page. When your browser receives a web page from a web server, it looks up the reference to a picture on the page and asks the web server to send the picture over. When it receives the picture, the browser positions it at the right place on the web page and then shows the web page to you.

Pictures take up more space than text. Naturally, they take up more bandwidth. As a result, a page takes longer to display in a browser as you add more pictures to it. Pictures certainly make a web page more attractive, but use them judiciously. Don't add unnecessary or meaningless pictures to your pages.

The larger the dimensions of a picture, the larger its file size is likely to be. You can reduce the file size by cropping unnecessary details from a picture. Reducing the file size of a picture without sacrificing picture quality appreciably is called *optimization*. Office Live Small Business's picture uploader has an optimization tool built in (as you'll see shortly). All you have to do is select a checkbox while uploading a picture. Make use of the feature whenever you can.

Pictures from digital cameras, especially high-resolution ones, are really huge. If you use them on web pages without cropping or optimizing them, your pages will take a long time to load in a browser. Therefore, the rule of thumb is to crop and optimize pictures in a tool, such as Photoshop, before using it on your web pages.

Although the Web is virtually an endless repository of pictures, they are protected by copyright law. Therefore, it's *not* okay to download random pictures and use them on your website. In the same vein, linking to pictures on other websites without the permission of their owners is also not an honest practice. Doing so amounts to stealing bandwidth.

Office Live Small Business stores all pictures that appear on your website in a special folder called **Image Gallery**. The tools you'll require to:

◆ upload pictures to the **Image Gallery**

◆ add references to those pictures from your web pages

◆ position the pictures where you want them on your web pages

are to be found, as you'd expect, in **Page Editor**.

Although this uploading-referencing-positioning business sounds really complicated, it's not. Let me show you how to do all of these tasks in a single stretch. Let's add a picture to my website. Presently, my **Home** page looks like this:

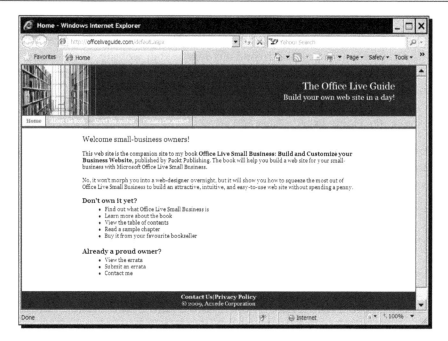

I want it to look like this:

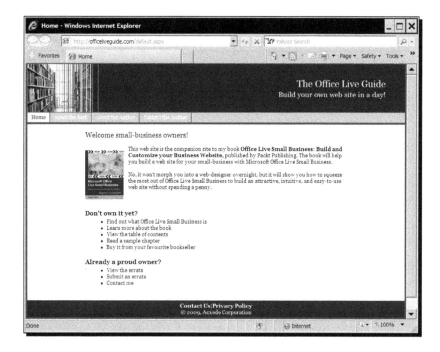

So, let's get cracking!

Time for action – displaying a picture

Because I don't know where you plan to add pictures to your website, I'll show you how to add one to mine. You can follow the same steps to add one to yours. Just use the appropriate page on your website as you work along with me.

1. Bring up the **Home** page in **Page Editor**.

2. Position the cursor where you want the picture to appear and click the **Image** button in the **Insert** group on **Page Editor**'s ribbon. The **Insert Image** dialog opens, as shown:

3. Choose the **My computer** radio button in the **Choose images from** radio button group in the left-hand side box.

4. Click the **Browse for an image...**button in the right-hand side box. The **Choose File to Upload** dialog opens, as shown:

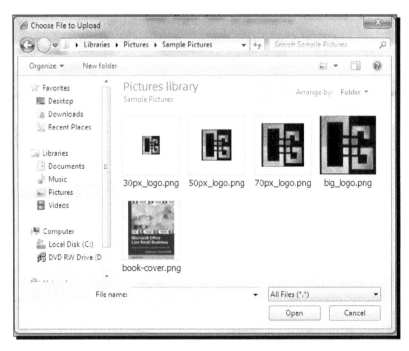

5. Navigate to the folder on your computer that contains the picture you want to upload by selecting it in the **Look in** dropdown. All the pictures in the folder will appear in the dialog.

6. Click the picture you want to upload. Its name appears in the **File name** textbox.

7. Click **Open**.

8. Then **Choose File to Upload** dialog closes. And a new checkbox, **Optimize my image**, appears in the **Insert Image** dialog. Check it if it's not already selected. When you do so, Office Live Small Business automatically reduces its file size as best as possible so that it downloads faster.

9. Click **Insert Image**. The **Insert Image** dialog goes away and the picture appears where your cursor was, as shown:

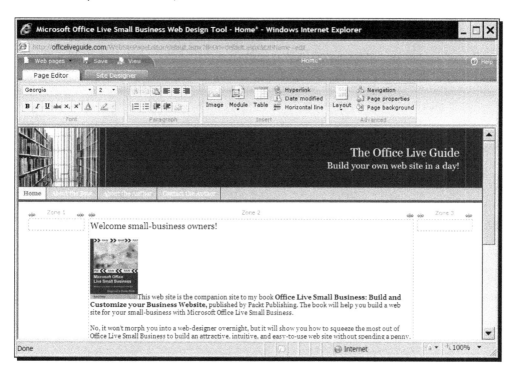

10. The problem, however, is that it sticks out like a sore thumb on the web page. It would look much better with the text wrapped around it. To make that happen, right-click on the image. A little action menu pops up, as shown:

11. Click **Float Left**. The action menu goes away and the text now wraps around the picture, as shown:

If you want to display the picture to the right of the paragraph, just click **Float Right** on the action menu.

12. Save your work and preview the page.

13. Close the preview window and return to **Page Editor**.

 How do you delete a picture?

Elementary, my dear Watson! Just click on it and hit the *delete* key on your keyboard.

What just happened?

You just learned how to make your web pages more attractive by displaying pictures to complement the text on them. Judicious use of pictures can enhance the appeal of your site tremendously.

But don't overdo it. Too many pictures not only clutter web pages, they also make the pages sluggish.

And here's a word of caution about working with pictures: when you select a picture in the **Page Editor**, square handles appear around it. These handles can be used to resize the picture. Don't use them. Pictures resized in this manner can end up looking kind of fuzzy or distorted. Instead, create the pictures with the right dimensions before uploading them to your web pages.

Have a go hero – working with pictures

Were you worried that your site looked awful without any pictures on it? Now that you know how to manipulate pictures, go ahead and add them in appropriate spots.

And here's a challenge for you. I'm sure that you've seen pictures that work like hyperlinks. When you click on them, they lead you to another web page. Can you make a picture on your web page behave the same way?

Hint: Right-click on the picture. You should see a **Create/edit hyperlink** *option on the menu that pops up.*

Presenting data in tabular format

So far, you've learnt how to add text to web pages, how to create hyperlinks, how to display images, and how to use modules with pre-programmed features. I'll now show you how to present data in a tabular format.

Time for action – creating a table

Just as with pictures, I don't know if or where you plan to present data using a table. So, we'll use the **Test** page that you created earlier. Once you know how to work with tables, you'll easily be able to add them to any of your pages.

1. Bring up the test page in **Page Editor**.

2. Position the cursor where you want to display the table and click the **Table** button in the **Insert** group on **Page Editor**'s ribbon. The **Create Table** dialog opens, as shown in the next screenshot:

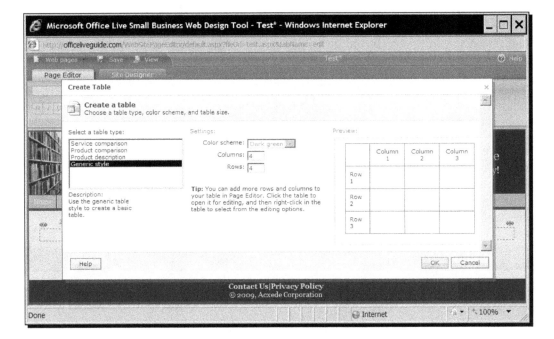

3. Select **Generic style** in the **Select a table type** box. Then, enter the number or columns and rows your table will have in the columns and rows textboxes, respectively. Don't worry if you don't know the exact number of rows or columns. You can always add or delete rows, as well as columns, from a table, even after you add it to a page, just as you would in a word processor.

   Why should you use **Generic style** when the other styles look more colorful?

There's a good reason. The colorful styles have colored backgrounds for alternate rows. That makes distinguishing between adjacent rows easier, as shown in the next image:

	Service 1	Service 2	Service 3
Area 1			
Area 2			
Area 3			

The problem, however, is that this color scheme breaks down if you add or delete rows from the table later on. That's because Office Live Small Business is not smart enough to adjust the backgrounds for alternate rows after you randomly hack at rows in the table. So, you might end up with tables like this:

	Service 1	Service 2	Service 3
Area 1			
Area 2			
Area 2			

Therefore, it's better to stick to the **Generic style**, which has white background for all rows.

4. Click **OK**. The **Create Table** dialog closes. A table now appears on the page where your cursor was, as shown:

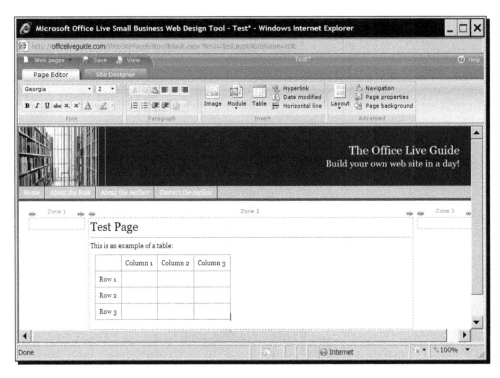

5. Right-click on the table. An action menu appears, as shown:

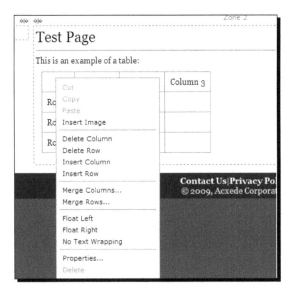

6. As you can see, it has commands to add rows, delete rows, merge rows and columns to create tables of virtually any internal shape. For example, the one below has three merged columns in **Row 1** and two merged rows in **Column 1**, as shown:

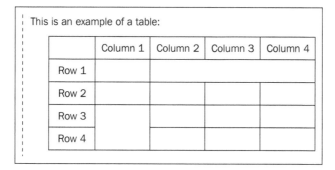

This is an example of a table:

	Column 1	Column 2	Column 3	Column 4
Row 1				
Row 2				
Row 3				
Row 4				

7. Go ahead and manipulate the table to your heart's content. After all, it's only a test page.

If you want to change the style of the table for any reason, click on **Properties...** on the action menu to bring up the **Create Table** dialog.

8. Save your work and preview the page.

9. Close the preview window and return to **Page Editor**.

How do you delete a table?

Surely, you know the drill by now. Select it with your mouse to reveal the picture's handles and hit the *delete* key on your keyboard.

What just happened?

You learned how to present data in a tabular format on your web pages. You learned how to add a table to your web page and how to manipulate and format its rows and columns.

If you're used to working with tables on a word processor or a spread sheet, you'll find Office Live Small Business's tables to be quite straightforward. The only thing that you should keep in mind is that they are not as sophisticated as their counterparts in word processors and spreadsheets. So, displaying complex tables with subtotals or subheadings might prove somewhat tricky.

Have a go hero – working with tables

Is the tabular format appropriate for presenting data on any of your web pages? A schedule of some sort, perhaps? Or a list of products and services or a thumbnail photo gallery? If so, now's the time to add those tables to your web pages.

Pop quiz 7.1

1. In Office Live Small Business's lingo, a module is:

    A. A way to connect two web pages through a hyperlink

    B. A pre-packaged mini-program that you can drop on a web page and configure it to perform a pre-determined task

    C. A structure to represent tabular data on a web page

2. Although it is possible to optimize pictures in Image Uploader, it's not a very good idea because optimized pictures make web pages sluggish. *True* or *false*?

3. Downloading pictures from other people's websites and using them on yours amounts to stealing. Therefore, you should hyperlink to those pictures instead. *Right* or *wrong*?

Summary

In this chapter, you made your website a bit more presentable. You learned how to use some of Office Live Small Business's modules, how to connect pages with hyperlinks, and how to add images and tables to make your pages more attractive and easy to read. To recap:

- **Page Editor** has several built-in mini-programs called modules. Modules allow you to add advanced features to your web pages without writing program code. You simply drop them on to a web page, set a few properties, and Office Live Small Business does the rest.

- Hyperlinks are just as easy to create. You select the text that you want to turn into a hyperlink and specify the web address of the resource that you want to link to.

- If you want to display pictures on your web pages, you must upload them to the **Image Gallery**. Once there, you can add them to any page and position them using the tools in **Page Editor**.

- You can present data in a tabular format using tables that work more or less like the tables in a word processor.

By now, you should have a complete website, more or less. In the next three chapters, you'll tweak some settings, add some custom code, improve the quality of the text on your pages, and do all those little things that will make your site look more polished.

8
Fine-tuning the Design

Let's face it: although you've built a great website with Office Live Small Business, you've only had a limited amount of control over your site's design elements so far. You chose a theme, a style, and a color scheme back in Chapter 2. That's pretty much it!

In this chapter, you'll learn how to go beyond those basic settings and make your site prettier. Specifically, you'll learn how to:

◆ Customize your site's header with a custom picture or your logo

◆ Customize your site's color scheme

◆ Use a custom stylesheet to fine-tune design elements

By the time you work your way through this chapter, your web pages will have a more professional look.

Customizing the header

Four design elements determine the look and feel of your site's header: logo, theme, style, and color scheme. When you set your site's design options back in Chapter 2, I advised you to tackle the logo later. But you did choose one of the available themes. You also chose a style that determines the layout of the header and a color scheme.

The extent to which you can control each of these four elements varies. At one end of the spectrum is the style. All you can do with it, is pick one of the available ones. The color scheme lies at the other end of the spectrum; you can customize it to your heart's content. The logo and the theme picture lie somewhere in the middle.

Recall from Chapter 2 that your site's theme is simply the picture that appears in its header. You just chose one of the many available pictures when you set the theme in **Site Designer**. You'll be happy to know that you're not limited to the pictures that Office Live Small Business supplies; you can supply your own pictures.

But there's a catch. Office Live Small Business automatically resizes your picture to fit in its style-and-theme structure. It may even apply special effects to it. Therefore, not every picture is suitable for a custom theme.

Office Live Small Business can accommodate a logo in the header as well. But there's a catch with it as well; you can control the size and location of the logo to an extent, but you can't position it in the header precisely where you want it; Office Live Small Business does it for you and the result is not always pretty.

One option, of course, is to use your logo as the picture for your custom theme but that's not really such a good idea. Photographs or abstract pictures generally tolerate Office Live Small Business's adjustments pretty well, but most logos don't. That's because logos tend to have letters or proportionate figures that promptly get distorted with the resizing and application of special effects.

Fortunately, that's not the end of the road. You have several options for customizing your website's header despite these limitations. It's a good idea, therefore, to know what those options are and how to choose one that's right for your website.

Here are the options then:

♦ A header with one of the pictures in a built-in theme

♦ A plain header without a logo or a picture

♦ A header with a picture of your choice

♦ A header with both your logo and a picture

♦ A header with only your logo in the header and no picture

Let's check these options one by one, so that you can choose the one that's most appropriate for your website.

While describing each of the options in detail below, I've provided general guidelines as to which option may be right for you, depending on your circumstances. But I suggest that you try out all the options possible before picking one.

A header with one of the built-in theme pictures

This option is appropriate for you if:

- ◆ You don't have a logo for your business
- ◆ You don't have a picture of your own to use in the header
- ◆ You can live with one of the built-in theme pictures

If you've followed along with me so far in this book, this is the option that your site is presently using. But even if you're happy with it, I suggest you read through the remaining options. Who knows? You may like another one better.

A plain header without a logo or a picture

This option is appropriate for you if:

- ◆ You don't have a logo for your business
- ◆ You don't like the way that Office Live Small Business displays pictures in the header
- ◆ You don't mind a relatively plain-looking header

Time for action – building a header without a logo or a picture

1. Go to **Site Designer** and pull down the themes menu by clicking on the **Themes** button on the ribbon.

2. Choose **General (no photos)**. The **Themes** menu goes away and the page currently displayed in the **Site Designer** displays the header's new design. My site looks something like this:

3. Pull down the **Style headers** menu by clicking on the **Style** button on the ribbon.

4. Try selecting each of the styles.

5. Choose the style that you like the best.

6. Save your work and preview the site.

What just happened?

You tried out a header without a logo for your website. As you can see, *no logo* doesn't mean *no images*; Office Live Small Business automatically displays abstract motifs in the header anyway. If you don't have a logo, this is one of the options that you should consider; Office Live Small Business often surprises you with attractive motifs.

A header with a picture of your choice

This option is appropriate for you if:

- You don't like any of the built-in pictures
- You have a picture that would go well in the header
- You're willing to experiment with the modifications that Office Live Small Business automatically makes to the picture

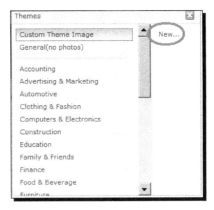

Time for action – building a header with a custom picture

1. Go to **Site Designer** and pull down the **Themes** menu by clicking on the **Theme** button on the ribbon.

2. Choose **Custom Theme Image**. A **New...** link appears in the right-hand pane of the **Themes** menu.

3. Click **New ....** The **Insert Image** dialog opens as shown:

4. You've seen this dialog before while uploading images in Chapter 7. Choose the **My computer** radio button in the left pane and upload the picture.

5. When it appears in the right pane, click on it to select it.

6. Click the **Insert image** button. The **Insert Image** dialog goes away and the page currently displayed in the **Site Designer** displays the header's new design. My site looks something like this:

7. Pull down the **Style headers** menu by clicking on the **Style** button on the ribbon.

8. Try selecting each of the styles. Notice how Office Live Small Business manipulates the images to go with the style.

9. Choose the style that you like the best.

10. Save your work and preview the site.

What just happened?

You learnt how to build a custom theme for your site. Although "custom theme" is just a grand name for uploading a picture of your choice, it is the option that you should consider for your site's header if you don't have a logo. But that doesn't mean that you shouldn't consider it even if you do have a logo. In the next section, you'll try out a header with both a logo and a picture.

A header with a logo and a picture

This option is appropriate for you if:

♦ You already have a logo

♦ You can find a picture that will go well alongside your logo in the header, either among those built-in, or in your own collection

♦ Considering that you don't have much control over their positioning, you're willing to manipulate them with Adobe Photoshop, or another similar program, in order to fit them into the header

Time for action – building a header with a logo and a picture

1. Go to **Site Designer**.

2. Make sure your site's header is showing either a built-in theme picture or a custom picture that you uploaded in the previous activity.

3. Click the **Header** button on the ribbon. The **Header** dialog opens.

4. Click on the **Logo** tab to display the logo information.

5. Click the **Upload pictures** button to upload the logo.

6. The now-familiar **Image Uploader** window pops up.

7. Upload the logo image. It appears in the **Header** dialog.

8. Click on the logo to select it as shown:

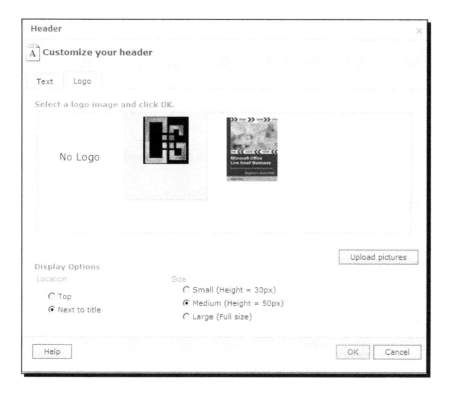

9. Choose the **Next to title** radio button.

10. Depending on how big your logo is, choose one of the radio buttons: **Small**, **Medium**, or **Large**, in the **Size** group.

11. Click **OK**.

12. The **Header** dialog goes away and the page currently displayed in the **Site Designer** displays the modified header with the logo. My site looks something like this:

13. Pull down the **Style headers** menu by clicking on the **Style** button on the ribbon.

14. Try selecting each of the styles. Notice how Office Live Small Business manipulates the position of the logo to go with the style.

15. Choose the style that you like the best.

16. Save your work and preview the site.

 Trying out the various styles gets a bit frustrating because the logo never quite appears in the position you'd like it to. But there's not much you can do about it other than selecting the one that you like the best from the lot.

What just happened?

You experimented with a header that sports a logo as well as a custom picture. As you can see, Office Live Small Business offers you several different ways of building your site's header. But even if you're happy with an option that you've already tried out, I urge you to try out the option in the next section before making the final decision.

A header with a logo but no picture

This option is appropriate for you if:

♦ You already have a distinctive logo

♦ Considering that you don't have much control over its positioning, you're willing to manipulate it with Adobe Photoshop or another similar program in order to fit it into the header

Time for action – building a header with a logo but no picture

1. Make sure you've completed the previous activity in order to have your logo available.

2. Go to **Site Designer** and pull down the **Themes** menu by clicking on the **Themes** button on the ribbon.

3. Choose **General (no photos)**. The **Themes** menu goes away and the page currently displayed in the **Site Designer** displays the header's new design.

4. Pull down the **Style headers** menu by clicking on the **Style** button on the ribbon.

5. Try selecting each of the styles.

6. Choose the style that you like the best. Here's the one that looks good for my site because Office Live Small Business gets the position of the logo just right:

7. Save your work and preview the site.

What just happened?

You cycled through the various ways of styling your website's header. As you've just experienced first-hand, styling the header is not an exact science. You may not be able to achieve the exact look that you had in mind but after some trial and error, there's a good chance that you'll hit upon a design you'll like.

Have a go hero – experiment with the header

If you're still not happy with the way the header looks, try this:

◆ Gather all pictures that you don't mind seeing in the header and your logo and upload them to your custom theme.

◆ If you have a logo, create several versions and sizes of it using Adobe Photoshop or your favorite graphics program, and upload them to your website.

Now, try out the various options again. When you encounter a design that would be acceptable to you except for some small detail, try using a different sized picture or logo. You can also try changing the face or the size of the font that you've set for the **Site Name** and **Site Slogan**.

Again, you may not achieve the exact look that you have in mind. But hey, there's much more to a website than just the header. So, get over it and choose one of those but-not-exactly-right designs that you like the best.

Although I have discussed several ways of designing your website's header using the built-in design tools, there are a couple more that require a more sophisticated approach:

♦ The first is to upload a picture that contains your site's name and slogan. I'll have to agree that the header can look much better than any that you can build using the built-in design tools.

However, there's a big downside to it. When you use such a picture, you have to get rid of the site name and site slogan in **Site Designer**. When you do so, search engines can't do a very good job of indexing your site and people are likely to have a harder time finding it using search engines. So, I don't recommend using it.

♦ The second option is to build a custom header using some of Office Live Small Business's **Advanced design features**. You can see an example at www.acxede.com. In a way, this is really the best option for your site's header. Unfortunately, it's meant for professional designers who, Microsoft hopes, will build for-sale designs that you can buy off-the-shelf. It requires you to know a few technologies that are more appropriate for programs rather than small-business owners. Still, if you know XML and XSLT, I have a brief tutorial on building custom headers on the book's companion website.

To cut a long story short, I recommend that you forget about these two options and choose one of the options that you've tried out in this chapter.

Pop quiz 8.1

1. Which design elements can you use to design your website's header simultaneously:

   A. A logo and a picture of your choice

   B. A site name and a picture of your choice

   C. A logo and a site name

   D. All of the above

Customizing the color scheme

In Chapter 3, you chose a color scheme for your website by selecting one of Office Live Small Business's many built-in color schemes in the **Site Designer** as shown:

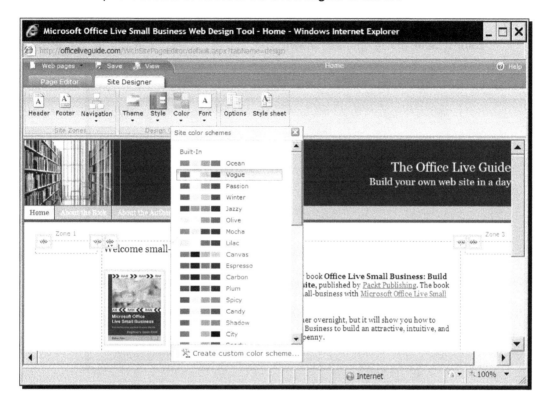

As we discussed then, these color schemes are designed by Microsoft's artists and they save you the trouble of coming up with your own. But, there are times when you're happy with a color scheme in general, although you'd be much happier if you could change a color or two. You'll be happy to know that Office Live Small Business gives you that ability.

Time for action – customizing the color scheme

1. Go to **Site Designer** and pull down the **Site color schemes** menu by clicking on the **Color** button on the ribbon.

2. Click the **Create custom color scheme** option at the very bottom. The **Edit custom color scheme** dialog opens as shown:

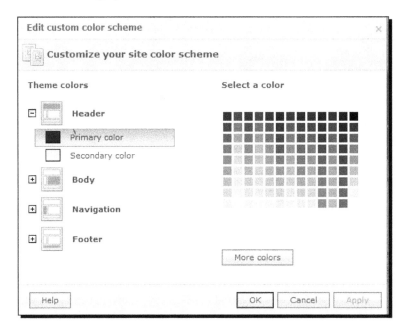

3. The colors in the scheme are grouped by their function and appear on the left-hand side of the dialog. You can see all the colors in a group by clicking on the little + and – signs before the group. The colors in the **Header**, for example, are **Primary color** and **Secondary color**. Select the color you want to change by expanding the appropriate group. An orange border appears around it to indicate the selection. I've selected **Primary color** for this example.

4. The color matrix on the right shows the colors that you have at your disposal. If none of these appeals to you, click the **More colors** button to reveal more colors.

5. Click on the color of your choice. It appears inside the orange border of the selected theme.

6. Click **OK**. The **Edit custom color scheme** dialog closes and you return to **Site Designer.**

7. Save your work and preview your website.

What just happened?

You learnt how to customize individual colors in the color scheme that you've chosen for your site. Although many of the built-in color schemes are very well co-ordinated, many people I've talked to, often don't like some particular color in a scheme. In earlier versions of Office Live Small Business, you couldn't customize individual colors. So, you had to resort to trickery.

Now that the option is available, I recommend taking advantage of it to build just the right color palette for your website.

Using a custom stylesheet

A stylesheet is a set of instructions that tells a web browser how to display the design elements on a web page. Normally, you'd have to create a stylesheet by hand when you build a website, but Office Live Small Business creates one for you automatically. As a matter of fact, almost every setting that you set in the **Site Designer** gets translated into the instructions that go in your site's stylesheet. When you set your site's default font to be **Georgia**, for example, Office Live Small Business created an instruction in your stylesheet.

Each such instruction is called a **style**. The good news is that you can tweak, or even over-ride, the styles that Office Live Small Business generates automatically for a more fine-grained control over your site's look and feel.

A complete course on stylesheets is way beyond the scope of this book, but I'll give you a taste of what you can do with custom styles.

Tweaking the navigation links

Building a website's navigation links manually is hard. Maintaining them over a period of time is even harder. Fortunately, Office Live Small Business builds and maintains the navigation links automatically for you behind-the-scenes, whenever you edit your web pages. But this convenience comes at a cost—you have very little control over how the links are displayed. Let me give you an example.

Look at the site's navigation in the following image when you have second-level web pages:

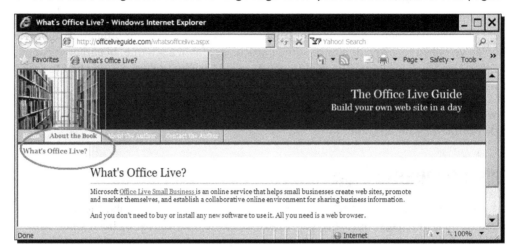

There are two problems with the navigation display I've highlighted:

♦ The second-level navigation link, **What's Office Live**, is displayed in a bigger font than the first-level navigation link, **About the Book**. While there's nothing wrong with this arrangement per-se, the second-level links can be mistaken for page or paragraph headers depending on the font, theme, and style that you choose.

♦ The second-level link's background is of the same color as the page background, not the same color as the rest of the second-level navigation bar. So, the link appears to be suspended in space and its purpose is not clear at first glance.

That's not all. There are a couple of other minor irritants that aren't obvious. Take a look at the behavior of a link in the following image when you hover your pointer over it:

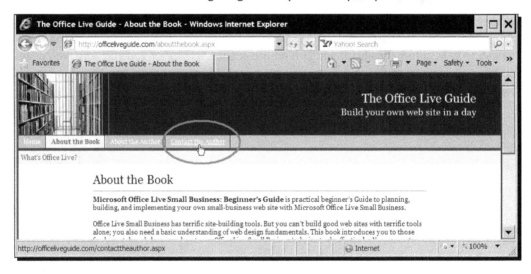

As you can see, an underline appears under the link. The trouble is that this behavior is not consistent. The underline appears only when a visitor has not visited the page. Once he does, the underline stops appearing during a hover. Therefore, some links on the navigation bar show the underline at any given time and others do not.

You may think that I'm making a mountain out of a mole hill, but one of the main reasons that a professionally-developed website looks, well... professional, is that someone charging big bucks has paid close attention to such trivialities throughout the site.

While these are not show-stoppers, you're better off doing something about them if you want your site to look professional. So, here's the plan of action. You'll:

♦ Use the font size for the first and second-level navigation links

♦ Make the links behave consistently on hover; always underline only on hover

♦ Make the background color of a selected second-level navigation link the same as the rest of the second-level navigation bar

The question, however, is: how do you do this? There are no settings for it in the **Site Designer** for sure. That's when your old friend, the stylesheet, comes to your rescue.

Recall that you used the stylesheet to set your site's width to 980 pixels back in Chapter 3. As you can see, your site's stylesheet gives you tremendous control over its look and feel.

Everything that you need to do here can be done with the stylesheet. But there's a small hitch! To remove the white background from the selected second-level navigation link, you must know the hexadecimal code for the background color of the second-level navigation bar. But, what exactly is a hexadecimal color code?

Every possible color has a unique numeric code. Although hexadecimal sounds like a really mean insult, it's not! It's just a number that uniquely identifies a specific color. It's written a bit differently though. In general, a hexadecimal color code begins with the pound sign(#) and has six more characters, each of which can range from 0-9 or a-f.

As a matter of fact, you don't have to know what a hexadecimal color code is. It's enough, for your purpose, to know what it looks like. The code for white is #ffffff, for example, and the code for black is #000000.

Hexadecimal color codes are not case-sensitive. So, #ffffff is the same thing as #FFFFFF, or #fFfFFf, for that matter. It's a good idea, however, to stick to all lowercase letters as I've done with the color codes in this chapter.

Although six characters follow the # in hexadecimal color codes, there's a shorthand notation that allows you to specify only three characters instead of six under certain conditions. So, don't be alarmed if you see a color code such as #fff. But to avoid confusion, at least initially, I recommend using all six characters.

There are many graphics tools that can help you to find the color of a given pixel on your screen. If you're familiar with one, use it to find the color code for the background color of the secondary navigation bar.

If you're not familiar with a graphics tool, you may want to try one of these:

Internet Explorer 8 has a built-in color picker tool that appears as a little floating dialog. It has a pointer that looks like an ink dropper. The color of the pixel at the pointer and its color code appear in the floating window. It looks something like this:

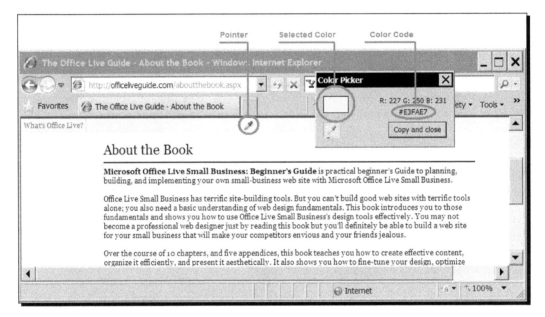

Complete instructions for using the color picker to find the code for a color are at http://www.officeliveguide.com/colorpicker.aspx. If you use a Windows computer, there's a great little freeware utility called *Pixie*. Like Internet Explorer 8's color picker, it too appears as a floating window, that contains the same information as shown in the following screenshot:

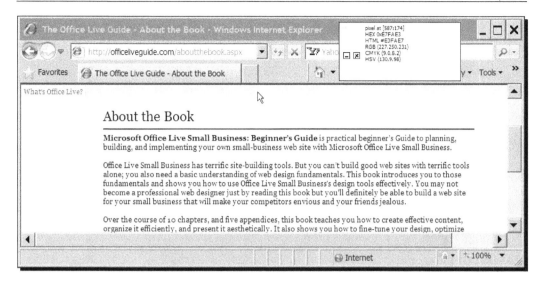

 Complete instructions for getting Pixie and using it to find the code for a color are at http://www.officeliveguide.com/colorpicker.aspx.

You'll use the graphics tool of your choice in the following activity.

Time for action – manipulating the stylesheet to fix the navigation

1. Go to **Page Manager** and preview your website.

2. Navigate to a page that has the second-level navigation bar.

3. Using a color picker tool, get the HTML code of the background color of the second-level navigation bar. Write it here: _____

4. Close the preview window and return to **Page Manager**.

5. Open the **Home** page in **Site Designer**.

6. Click on the **Style Sheet** button on the ribbon. The **Style Sheet** dialog opens as shown:

7. Type the following code below what's already there:

You must be very careful while typing this code. Every dot, colon, comma, underscore, and parenthesis is significant. One small error and your page will end up looking weird. To make your life easier, I've posted the code at http://www.officeliveguide.com//customstyles.aspx. I suggest you simply copy and paste it.

```
.MSC_SecondaryNavLink, .MSC_SecondaryNavLink:hover,
.MSC_SecondaryNavLink:visited, .MSC_SecondaryNavLink-On,
.MSC_SecondaryNavLink-On:hover, .MSC_SecondaryNavLink-On:visited
{ font-size:12px;}

.MSC_PrimaryNavLink:visited:hover, .MSC_SecondaryNavLink:visited:hover
{ font-size:12px; text-decoration:underline; }

.MSC_SecondaryNavLink-On, .MSC_SecondaryNavLink-On:visited,
.MSC_SecondaryNavLinkFrame-On
{background: #XXXXXX}
```

8. In the last line, carefully replace #XXXXXX with the color code that you noted down earlier. For my website, it is **#e3fae7**, which is what you see in the picture above.

9. Click **OK**. The **Style sheet** dialog closes.

10. Save your work and preview your website to ensure that the navigation now works the way you want it to.

11. Close the preview window and return to **Site Designer**.

You'll be doing a good bit of work with stylesheet in this chapter. As you've just revisited the **Style Sheet** dialog after first encountering it in Chapter 3, I'll skip the instructions for bringing the dialog up from now on. I'll simply say open the **Style Sheet** dialog and type such and such code, instead of repeating the instructions for opening it every time.

What just happened?

You just addressed all of the little issues about your website's navigation and polished it up.

But what if you want to do only a part of what I suggested? No problem. I've arranged the code in three visual chunks. Let's see what each chunk does:

- The first chunk makes the font size for all navigation links the same:

  ```
  .MSC_SecondaryNavLink, .MSC_SecondaryNavLink:hover,
  .MSC_SecondaryNavLink:visited, .MSC_SecondaryNavLink-On,
  .MSC_SecondaryNavLink-On:hover, .MSC_SecondaryNavLink-On:visited
  { font-size:12px;}
  ```

  If you don't want to do this on your website, bring up the **Style Sheet** dialog and delete this chunk.

- The second chunk makes the underlining on hover for the primary navigation consistent:

  ```
  .MSC_PrimaryNavLink:visited:hover, .MSC_SecondaryNavLink:visited:
  hover { font-size:12px; text-decoration:underline; }
  ```

  If you don't want to do this on your website, bring up the **Style Sheet** dialog and delete this chunk.

- The third chunk makes the underlining on hover for the secondary navigation consistent:

  ```
  .MSC_SecondaryNavLink-On, .MSC_SecondaryNavLink-On:visited,
  .MSC_SecondaryNavLinkFrame-On
  {background: #XXXXXX}
  ```

  If you don't want to do this on your website, bring up the **Style Sheet** dialog and delete this chunk.

I've arranged the code above in a way that a chunk of code achieves a single objective. With this arrangement, you can simply ignore a chunk of code if you choose not to implement something on your website.

Just to let you know, this is not the most efficient way of working with a stylesheet. It
results in some unnecessary duplication of code and increases the size of the stylesheet, which is not really a good thing. But in some circumstances, understandable code is preferable to efficient, or even clever code. When you're not a stylesheet guru, you're
in one of those circumstances.

But if, by any chance, you know your way around styles, feel free to use the class and instance identifiers in the code to rearrange it in anyway that you want to. And if you don't really know what that means, stick to my version of the code.

Displaying borders around pictures

Pictures look better when they're in frames. That's true on web pages too. Take the picture on my **Home** page, for example:

It appears to be floating randomly on the page. It will look much better if I put a frame around it like this:

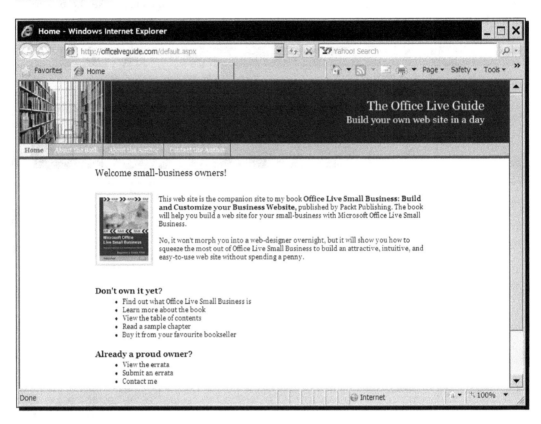

Doesn't that look much better? Let me show you how to achieve that effect.

Time for action – displaying a border around pictures

1. Open the **Style Sheet** dialog.

2. Type the following code what's already there:

 I've posted the code at `http://www.officeliveguide.com/ customstyles.aspx` if you want to just copy and paste it.

```
#IWS_WH_Elem_Content img {border: 4px solid #cccccc; padding: 5px;}
```

3. Save your work and preview your website. Every picture on your site should now have a border.

4. Close the preview window and return to **Site Designer**.

What just happened?

You styled the pictures on your website to display a pretty border around them. Mind you, the style adds a border to *all* pictures on the site, not just one.

What if I want a border around only some of the pictures?

With this technique, it's all-or-nothing. To display or remove a border around a single picture, you'll need to ability to manipulate styles on that picture. Unfortunately, Office Live Small Business doesn't offer you the ability to do so.

There certainly are ways to achieve that effect if push comes to shove, but none of them are fool-proof. There're either too complex for beginners or have unintended side effects.

Have a go hero – play with styles

Does the code that I've presented so far look esoteric to you? It just might. But come to think of it, it's not all that complex. Of course, there are rules that you must abide by, but you can take a chance and tweak it a bit. Take the code that you just used, for example:

```
#IWS_WH_Elem_Content img {border: 4px solid #cccccc; padding: 5px;}
```

When working with styles in Office Live Small Business, you're better off not touching anything outside the braces. So, let's concentrate on the stuff inside them:

```
border: 4px solid #cccccc; padding: 5px;
```

Translated into English, it says:

Draw a solid border, 4 pixels thick, in the color represented by the code #cccccc. And while you're at it, also pad the picture with 5 pixels of empty space on all sides so that the border is separated from the picture.

It should now be easy enough for you to customize the properties of the border. Want to make it thicker or thinner? Change 4 to whatever number of pixels you want. Want to change the color? Change #cccccc to your favourite color. The padding too much or too little for your liking? Change 5 to whatever number of pixels you want it to be.

By the way, I've chosen #cccccc as the border's color because it's a shade of grey that goes with most pictures. But that's my opinion. If you don't like it, try making it the same as the background of your site's header.

Styling horizontal rules

When you created your site template, you added a horizontal line under the page header. These lines are called *horizontal rules* in HTML. The way browsers display horizontal rules, *hr* in short, is not always pretty. Internet Explorer, for example, displays it as a three-dimensional grey line. You can make it look prettier by assigning a color to it.

There's no hard and fast rule as to what the color should be, but it's often a good idea to choose one of the colors in your site's color scheme. You can get the code for that color by using your favorite color picker.

Time for action – styling the horizontal rules

1. Open the **Style Sheet** dialog.

2. Type the following code below what's already there:

    ```
    hr { color: #XXXXXX; }
    ```

    I've posted the code at `http://www.officeliveguide.com/customstyles.aspx` if you want to just copy and paste it.

3. Carefully replace #XXXXXX with the color code of your choice. For my website, it is #333399, which is what you see on the companion website.

4. Save your work and preview your website. Every horizontal rule on your site should now have the color that you assigned rather than the default grey.

5. Close the preview window and return to **Site Designer**.

    You can do quite a few little things with styles. You can change the color of navigation links, for example, or change the way that bullets in a bulleted list look. I've posted a list at http://www.officeliveguide.com/customstyles.aspx. I'll be updating it from time to time. So, I encourage you to look it up once in a while.

What just happened?

You styled the horizontal rules on your website. They will now appear as pretty solid lines of the color of your choice, instead of their default grey. As with the pictures, the style changes the color of *all* horizontal rules on the site; not just one.

Pop quiz 8.2

1. Which of the following is NOT a valid hexadecimal color code?

    A. #ffffff

    B. #A0b0c0

    C. #aaaggg

    D. #999999

Summary

In this chapter, you learnt how to fine-tune several of your site's design elements. After working through it, you should find Office Live Small Business's design options a lot less restrictive than they initially appear. To recap:

- Every Office Live Small Business theme has a set of pictures. One of them appears in your site's header. If you don't like any of them, you can supply your own.

- Displaying a logo in your website's header is a bit tricky. Office Live Small Business has limited options for positioning it. Therefore, placing it at precisely a certain location in the header is hard. But even if none of the available styles displays it to your liking, you can control its display, somewhat, by adjusting its size.

- You may not be able to get your site's header to look exactly as you want it to. But with sufficient trial and error, you should be able to make it look acceptably pretty.

- You can customize the color scheme that Office Live Small Business applies to your site using a built-in color picker tool.

- Although Office Live Small Business automatically generates a stylesheet for your website, you can over-ride styles for some of the elements. I showed you how to use styles to tweak your site's navigation links, decorate pictures on your site with borders, and style horizontal rules. But that's not all; you can do much more. I've created a more comprehensive list on this book's companion site that you can use to tweak your site's stylesheet even more.

Although you focused on your site's design elements in this chapter, its content is as important to its ultimate success as its design, if not more. In the next chapter, you'll focus on fine-tuning the content—for search engines as well as people.

9

Venturing Beyond the Basics

Office Live Small Business is the perfect site-building tool for you if you don't know (or don't want to learn) HTML, the language of web pages. And I'm sure that you'll agree that it does a pretty decent job of it. But after your site is functionally complete, it's only natural that you'd want to tweak little things here and there; move the text on some page a wee bit to the left, for example, or move a picture up by a pixel or two, so as to align it with the neighboring text. The trouble, though, is that Office Live Small Business doesn't allow such tweaks. You can't touch the HTML that it generates.

But what if you're not very happy with this state of affairs? Don't worry! Office Live Small Business has it covered. It has two advanced features that give you a fine-grained control over the look and feel of your web pages as follows:

- **Page Editor**'s *HTML modules* in which you can write your own HTML markup
- Off-the-shelf *Solutions*, which render customized web pages within Office Live Small Business's framework

In this chapter, you'll explore both these advanced options. Here's what you'll do:

- Add an HTML module to your page.
- Write HTML in the HTML module. Chances are that you don't know a lot about HTML. So, you'll take a crash course on a small subset of HTML that will help you to get started with writing your own markup, if you so desire.
- Perform some common page-building tasks such as embedding flash movies, PayPal buttons, and other such external content in your web pages using the HTML module.
- Download and install an FAQ solution that renders a customized FAQ page.

Let's get started then.

About HTML modules

An HTML module is a little editor that you can plop on to your page in the **Page Editor**, just like any other module. It holds HTML markup. With an HTML module, you can construct a web page with raw HTML markup just as the pros do.

If you're conversant with HTML, the idea of having a fine-grained control over your HTML is likely to pump you up. And yet, I don't recommend using HTML modules.

You read that right: *I don't recommend using HTML modules*. Why? Because Office Live Small Business stores the markup in HTML modules separate from the page. When a person requests your page from his/her browser, Office Live Small Business fetches the separately-stored markup and embeds it into the rest of the page dynamically. The problem is that it does the embedding using something called *frames*, which happen to be little windows on a web page that display content that doesn't actually reside on that page.

Why is this problematic? Because search engines can't index the content that doesn't physically reside on your web page. Therefore, people can't find it using search engines. Frankly, I don't see a point in building a site that people can't find. So, I strongly discourage you to build your entire site with HTML modules.

Another reason to avoid HTML modules is that they load the content dynamically using JavaScript. This can be an excruciatingly slow process that can delay the loading of a page in a user's browser. In fact, such dynamically loaded pages often tend to time out.

Having said that, there are situations where they can come in handy. You may not care, for example, whether search engines index a certain page on your site, but you'd like to have great control over how that page looks. Or you may want to embed a YouTube video on your page, which search engines don't index any way. It's a good idea, therefore, to learn how to use the HTML module and that's what you'll do in this section.

The first step, of course, is to add an HTML module to one of your pages. Let's use the **Test** page that you created in Chapter 7.

Time for action – adding an HTML module to your page

1. Bring up the **Test** page in **Page Editor**.

2. Place the cursor where you want to add the module.

3. Click the **Module** button in the **Insert** group on the **Page Editor**'s ribbon. Select **HTML** from the **Modules** menu that drops down. The **HTML** dialog pops up, as shown:

The dialog contains a mini-editor where you can type your HTML markup. The **Images** and **Hyperlink** buttons just above the editor box help you add markup for embedding pictures and hyperlinks. As this is just a **Test** page, I'll type some simple HTML to show you how the module really works. I suggest that you do the same.

4. Type the following markup in the mini-editor:

    ```
    <strong>Welcome to my web site.</strong>
    ```

5. Click **OK**. The **HTML** dialog closes and you return to **Page Editor**, which renders the HTML you just typed as any browser would.

6. Preview your website. The page should now look like this:

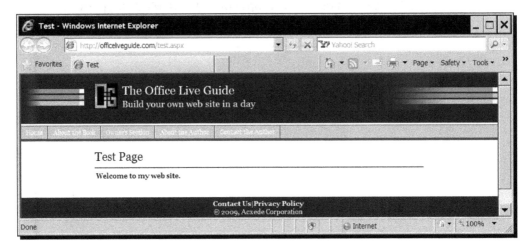

7. Close the preview window and return to **Page Editor**.

8. Editing your markup is equally easy. Right-click on the HTML module in **Page Editor**. A pop-up menu appears, as shown in the next image:

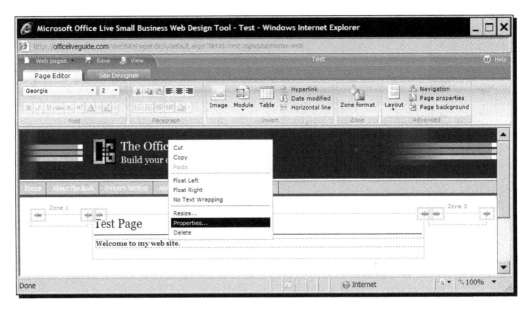

9. Choose **Properties....** the **HTML** dialog opens again with your markup in it. Change the markup to:

```
<strong>Welcome</strong> to my web site.
```

You'll be working with the HTML module a few more times in this chapter. From now on, I'll just say "Open the HTML module's HTML dialog" when I want you to edit a module's markup.

10. Click **OK**. The **HTML** dialog closes and you return to **Page Editor**.

11. Preview your website. The page should now display only the word **Welcome** in bold letters.

12. Close the preview window and return to **Page Editor**.

What just happened?

You added an HTML module to a web page and typed some basic HTML in it.

Before this exercise, you simply typed text on to your web pages as you would in a word processor, and Office Live Small Business took care of converting it to HTML. With an HTML module, you're writing your own HTML. Naturally, you'll have a more fine-grained control over how you want it to appear. But to make use of this newfound power, you must know HTML. So, let me give you a brief tutorial on it.

There are several hundred excellent HTML tutorials on the Web (not to mention several thousand lousy ones). If you take into account the hundreds of books on the subject, you'd think that everything that needs to be said about HTML has, perhaps, already been said. Many times over, at that.

Yet, I have good reason to write this brief tutorial: writing HTML for Office Live Small Business web pages is an entirely different beast.

Why? Because:

◆ You don't write an entire HTML document with Office Live Small Business's design tools. All you do is write little chunks of HTML in HTML modules placed strategically on your web pages. Office Live Small Business's **Page Editor** combines the basic framework of your web page with these chunks of HTML and presents a finished web page to your browser.

◆ An HTML module doesn't store the HTML you type verbatim. It encodes what you type and lets the browser handle the decoding. Therefore, the page may not look exactly as you intend it to, after the browser renders it.

◆ The page on which you drop an HTML module already has a **Cascaded Style Sheet (CSS)** associated with it. You may be able to take advantage of the fact and minimize manual formatting.

Therefore, you don't have to be an HTML guru to use Office Live Small Business's HTML module. All you need to know is a small subset of HTML that leverages the web page's features. This tutorial introduces that subset. It won't make you a fully-fledged web designer, but it will arm you with enough knowledge to impress unsuspecting folks at cocktail parties.

HTML 101

Contrary to what many people believe, HTML is not a programming language. It's a markup language. Unlike programming languages, it doesn't contain step-by-step instructions that tell a computer what to do. Instead, it contains instructions that tell a browser how to format and decorate web page content.

The instructions are written as *Tags*. Tags are keywords that reside within a pair of angular brackets (< and >). Typically, you enclose some content between a pair of tags.

For example, the `<strong>` and `</strong>` in the markup you just tried out is tag pair. The pair consists of an opening tag and a closing tag. The difference between an opening tag and the corresponding closing tag is usually a forward slash (/). So, `<strong>` is the opening tag and `</strong >` is the corresponding closing tag. If you want to make some text bold, you enclose it between `<strong>` and `</strong>` tags like this:

```
This is some text. <strong>This sentence is bold.</strong> This one
isn't.
```

And the browser displays it like this:

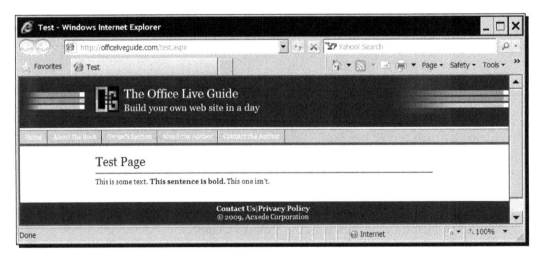

Most HTML tags are paired like the `<strong>` tag. But some are not. An example is the `<br />` tag. It adds a line break to your text like this:

```
This is some text. <br /> This is some more text but it's on the next
line.
```

And the browser displays it like this:

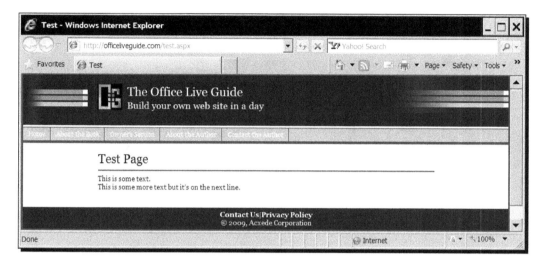

The character `<` opens the tag and the character sequence `/>` closes it. Such tags that close themselves without corresponding closing tags are called self-closing tags. It's not mandatory to close the self-closing tags. So, if you write `<br>` instead of `<br />`, your page will work just fine. But I recommend closing all tags. I'll do so in this tutorial and so will you.

Notice, by the way, that simply typing the second line of text on a new line in the editor doesn't make the text appear on the next line (go ahead, try it!). It's the `<br />` tag that actually does the trick and displays the subsequent text on the next line, although you typed it as a single line in the editor. In other words, the tags determine the appearance of your web page, not how you type the text in the editor.

HTML is not case sensitive. So, you can write a `<br />` tag as `<BR />`, `<Br />`, or even `<bR />`, if you insist, and your page won't look any different. But, I strongly advise against it. As a matter of convention, I recommend sticking to lowercase letters, as I've done throughout this tutorial.

That's just about all the dirt that you really need to know on HTML. There's more, of course, but as this is not a complete HTML tutorial, we'll look into the finer details on a need-to-know basis. So, let's proceed to some useful HTML tags.

Working with paragraphs

Most writing is structured as a collection of paragraphs. While writing HTML, you must enclose the text in a paragraph between the `<p>` and `</p>` tag pair like this:

```
<p>This is the first paragraph. It has this filler text to make it
rather long so that it looks like a real paragraph.</p><p>Here is the
second paragraph.</p>
```

And the browser renders it like this:

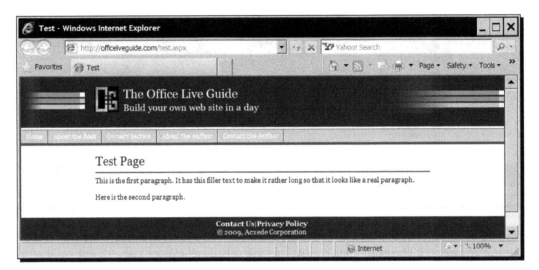

As you can see, there's no space between the paragraphs in the markup. But the `<p></p>` tag pair automatically introduces breaks that makes the text look like paragraphs in the browser.

Because of a bug in the HTML module, it doesn't seem to treat `<p>` and `</p>` tags correctly. As a result, you don't see intended paragraph breaks in the browser. In the picture above, I sneaked in our old friend, the `<br />` tag, between the two paragraphs as in `<p>...</p> <br /> <p>...</p>`.

You may have to resort to this workaround as well. But remember that if Microsoft fixes the bug, you'll get an extra line-break on your page.

Also, remember that you can add text to an HTML module without the paragraph tag pair; you can use `<br />` tags instead, for example, where you want a break in text. However, I recommend that you enclose all of your text in paragraph tags. If you don't, Office Live Small Business's stylesheets may hijack the formatting of your text. Not enclosing text in paragraphs is one of the main reasons why text on so many web pages is misaligned and displayed in the wrong font.

Working with horizontal rules

Back in Chapter 5, I introduced the horizontal line, which you can draw across your web page simply by clicking the **Horizontal line** button on **Page Editor**'s ribbon. To draw a similar line while working with the HTML module, you'll need—you guessed it—a tag! Web designers call a horizontal line a horizontal rule and so the corresponding tag is the `<hr />` tag, like the `<br />` tag, the `<hr />` tag. Simply type `<hr />` wherever you want a horizontal line to appear. If you want it to appear between the two paragraphs in the previous example, your markup will look like this:

```
<p>This is the first paragraph. It has this filler text to make it
rather long so that it looks like a real paragraph.</p><hr /><p>Here
is the second paragraph.</p>
```

And your page will appear in the browser like this:

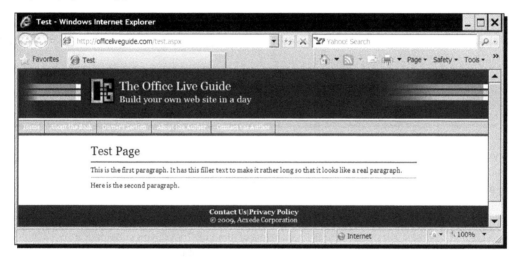

Working with headings

Headings are an important part of the text. Books, for example, use headings with varying importance. The more important a heading, the bigger its font size is. This scheme makes it easy for readers to quickly grasp the scope of topics and sub-topics within the text.

HTML uses a similar scheme. There are six levels of heading tag pairs in HTML that you can put around heading text like this:

```
<h1>Heading 1</h1>
<h2>Heading 2</h2>
<h3>Heading 3</h3>
<h4>Heading 4</h4>
<h5>Heading 5</h5>
<h6>Heading 6</h6>
```

Text included between beginning and ending tags at each level looks like this:

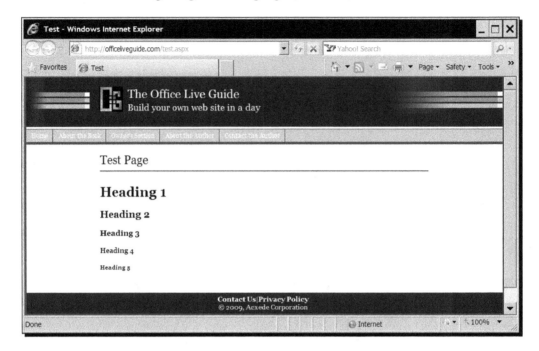

As you can see, `<h1>` has the largest font size. Naturally, it's used for the most important heading on a web page. As the number inside the tag increases, its font size decreases. So, among headings, `<h6>` has the smallest font size.

What if you need more than six levels of headings? Well, you shouldn't; a six level deep topic hierarchy is deep enough for most people to keep track of. If you have seven or more levels, you should seriously consider rewriting your text.

Generally, it's a good idea to start a page with the `<h1>` tag. It identifies the most important heading on the page, and it is used by search engines to take an educated guess at what the page is all about. So, a good convention to follow is to have only one `<h1>` tag on every web page.

But, you're better off flouting this convention when working with Office Live Small Business. Why? Because you don't write entire web pages in HTML modules; you just write individual chunks of HTML. Office Live Small Business automatically adds a `<h1></h1>` tag pair to your web pages and places the title of your site between them. Similarly, it uses the `<h2></h2>` tag pair for your site's tag line. So, you're better off starting with a `<h3>` tag in every HTML module on a web page. That way, you won't drive Google's spider nuts by forcing it to wrestle with 23 `<h1>` tags on a single web page.

When you need a sub-heading on the page, you should use the next tag down in the hierarchy; in our example, `<h4>`. Avoid the temptation to skip levels. Don't jump from `<h3>` to `<h6>`, for example. And it's a good idea to use these heading tags. Don't just write plain text with large fonts instead.

Working with hyperlinks

The HTML tags that you've seen so far merely alter the appearance of the text that they enclose. They're quite easy to work with. Just enclose some text between them and they alter its appearance. But all HTML is not that straightforward. You need more complex markup to perform more complex tasks.

Creating a hyperlink, for example, requires slightly more involved markup. It's not rocket science, but even a small mistake in the markup can leave your hyperlink broken. To prevent you from inadvertently creating broken hyperlinks, the HTML module's mini-editor lends you a helping hand. It lets you create the markup precisely in the same manner as you did outside of it.

Let's say you want to build a web page using an HTML module, which looks like this:

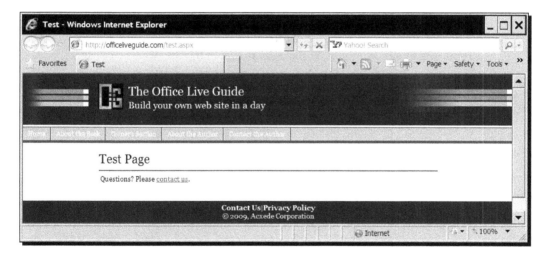

The question is, how do you write the markup for the **Contact Us** link? Well, I could easily tell you that the markup should look like this:

```
<a href="/contactus.aspx">contact us</a>
```

But as you can see, I'd have to give you a good amount of explanation as to what **href** means and why it's enclosed within a pair of double quotes. Then, some of you may want to know what happens if you omit the double quotes. So, one thing would lead to another and you would find yourself spending all of your time learning the nuances of HTML, rather than doing whatever it is that you do for a living.

So, the HTML module has a feature that writes the markup for you. Let me walk you through it.

Time for action – generating the markup for a hyperlink

1. Bring up the **Test** page in **Page Editor**. It should have the HTML module that you added just a short while ago. (Add another one if it isn't there any more.)

2. Open its **HTML** dialog. Clear any markup that might already be there and type:

   ```
   <p>Questions? Please contact us.</p>
   ```

3. Select the text **contact us** and click the **Hyperlink** button just above the mini-editor.

4. The **Insert a link** dialog opens. You've seen this dialog before. It pops up every time you insert a hyperlink outside of the HTML module using the **Hyperlink** button on **Page Editor**'s ribbon.

5. Choose the **Page on my site** radio button in its left pane. A list of all the pages on your site appears in the right pane, as shown in the following screenshot:

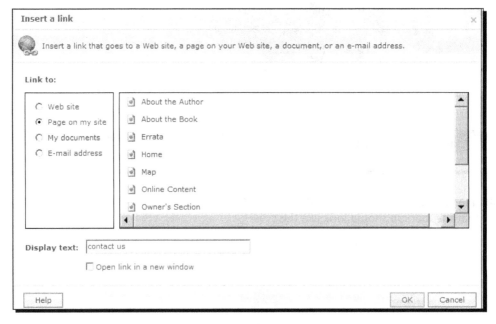

6. Select your contact page and click **OK**. The **Insert a link** dialog closes and you return to the HTML dialog.

7. Notice that the text in the editor now looks like this:

`Questions? Please <a href="/contactus.aspx" >contact us</a>.`

As you can see, Office Live Small Business added the necessary markup for you.

8. Click **OK** to close the HTML dialog and return to **Page Editor**.

9. Preview your site and confirm that the hyperlink works as intended.

What just happened?

The HTML module generated HTML markup for you at the click of a button! Come to think of it, this is exactly how Office Live Small Business works behind-the-scenes. When you create a hyperlink, add a horizontal line, or format pretty much any text in **Page Editor**, it generates the necessary HTML markup so that you don't have to learn HTML. The only difference here is that you actually get to see the markup.

Working with pictures

You might have noticed that in the **HTML** dialog, there's an **Images** button right next to the **Hyperlink** button that you just used to magically generate the hyperlink markup. Any guesses what that's for? Yes, it generates the markup necessary to display a picture on your web page.

As is the case with the **Hyperlink** button, the **Images** button works exactly the same way within the HTML module as it does outside of it.

Have a go hero – experiment with a picture's HTML markup

You've used the **Images** button in Chapter 7 to insert images on to your web pages. Can you now generate the markup in the HTML module to display a picture?

Working with external content

Some of the most common elements on many websites don't actually reside on those websites. Take a YouTube video, for example, a blog hosted at Blogger, or even an Amazon aStore. People commonly display such elements from external services on their web pages. How do you do that?

Well, all of these services provide you with HTML markup that is specific to that content and ask you to paste it on to your web page. On your Office Live Small Business website, you must paste it into an HTML module.

Why can't I paste it on the page itself?

Because what you're pasting is markup, not text. If you paste a YouTube video's markup in **Page Editor**, the web page will display the markup, not the video.

To give you an example, I created a small video clip and uploaded it to YouTube. To display it on my web page, YouTube informs me that I must use the following markup:

```
<object width="425" height="344"><param name="movie"
value="http://www.youtube.com/v/j5HoGG767MQ&hl=en&fs=1&"></
param><param name="allowFullScreen" value="true"></param><param
name="allowscriptaccess" value="always"></param><embed src="http://
www.youtube.com/v/j5HoGG767MQ&hl=en&fs=1&" type="application/x-
shockwave-flash" allowscriptaccess="always" allowfullscreen="true"
width="425" height="344"></embed></object>
```

To display this clip on my web page, all I have to do is to paste this markup in an HTML module on my page. I did so, and here's what my page looks like:

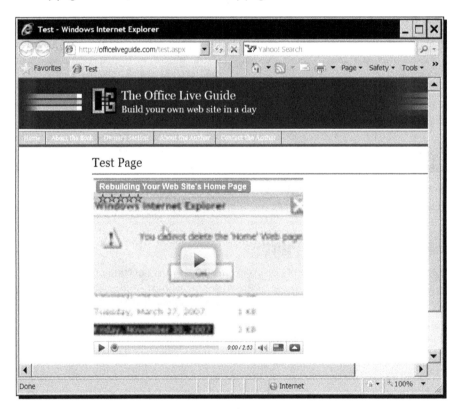

And while we're on the subject, you can also embed JavaScript into an HTML module. Some services, such as Google's AdSense advertising service, require you to embed JavaScript code, as opposed to HTML markup, into your web pages. HTML modules let you do that seamlessly.

 Although AdSense has a cult following, advertisements make sense only on news portals, online magazines, and such. They don't have a place on small-business websites. Displaying AdSense advertisements on your small-business websites is like displaying your competitor's billboard in your office. Don't do it!

Have a go hero – experiment with a picture's HTML markup

Do you have something hosted at a service such as YouTube, Amazon, or Blogger that you'd like to display on your web page? If so, give it a shot. Simply plop an HTML module on the page on which you want the content to appear, copy the markup from the service's website, and paste it into the HTML module.

Don't have any such hosted content? You can try it out using my YouTube video clip. You can copy the code from YouTube's site.

1. Point your browser at `http://www.youtube.com/watch?v=j5HoGG767MQ` as shown:

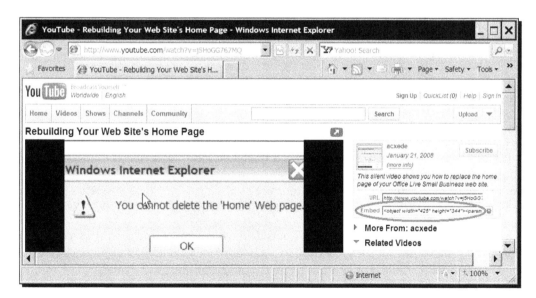

2. Copy the code in the little **Embed** box on the right and paste it in your HTML module.

Most services will provide you the markup in a similar fashion.

 As I mentioned before, you can embed all sorts of external content using HTML modules. Go to this book's companion website at http://www.officeliveguide.com/externalcontent.aspx to see more examples.

Pop quiz 9.1

1. HTML contains instructions on:
    A. Formatting the text and other content on a web page
    B. Configuring Office Live Small Business modules
    C. All of the above
    D. None of the above

2. You found this HTML markup on a web page:

   `<strong>elephant</strong>.`

   What do you think the markup does?

    A. It states that an elephant is strong at one end and extra-strong at the other
    B. It displays the word **elephant** in bold letters when the web page is displayed in a browser
    C. All of the above
    D. None of the above

Further customization with solutions

Now that you've seen the power of HTML modules, let me introduce you to yet another way of taking control of your web pages: *solutions*.

The common denominator of everything that you've done so far in **Site Designer** and **Page Editor** is that you created every page on your site using Office Live Small Business's page templates. Then, you just manipulated the content on the page.

But is it possible to build entire web pages outside of your website and then simply stick them in to your website? It certainly is. Such a web page, or a set of web pages packaged together as a unit, is called a solution in Office Live Small Business's parlance.

You can't, however, take any random web page and make it a part of your website. You must build one from scratch and you must follow a complex list of rules while building it, so that it can function within Office Live Small Business's framework. That, obviously, is not an item on the to-do list of small-business owners. You'd need hard-core programmers for the job.

Microsoft developed the Office Live Small Business platform as an extensible platform for independent software vendors to build solutions that would help small-business owners take all the aspects of their businesses online. One vendor may build a payroll system on the platform, for example, and another may build an inventory control system. Although there aren't all that many solutions out there as yet, you can expect to see more of them in the future. Microsoft hopes that vendors will create such solutions for various aspects of a business that you'll buy off-the-shelf and drop on to your web pages.

To give you a taste of the punch that solutions can pack, I've created a simple FAQ system. Office Live Small Business's FAQ page template leaves much to be desired. You can't have more than ten questions, for example, and it's very easy to mess up its formatting irreversibly. My FAQ system, called AcxedeFAQ, fixes these problems. You can create as many questions and answers as you want, and they always retain their formatting. All you have to do to use it, is download it and install it on your website. You'll find the downloadable package and complete instructions on installing and using AcxedeFAQ at `http://www.officeliveguide.com/AcxedeFAQ.aspx`.

Summary

In this chapter, you learnt that Office Live Small Business lets you go beyond its point-and-click tools and lets you customize the HTML markup of your web pages. It also allows you to install compatible web pages developed by third-party vendors. To recap:

- The HTML module is just another module in **Page Editor**, but it's unique in that it lets you actually write HTML markup like the pros do.
- You can write just about any valid HTML markup in an HTML module.
- I gave you a brief tutorial on HTML that's very specific to what you can expect to do with an HTML module. Of course, it's just a start. If you're an advanced HTML author, you can write as complex a markup as you want.
- HTML modules can also take scripts that let you embed external content such as blogs, videos, and even advertisements on your web pages.
- Although HTML modules appear to be the solution to all your site customization problems, you should use them only occasionally because search engines can't index content within them.
- Solutions are ready-made add-ons that you can install on your website. There aren't all that many of them out there as yet, but you can expect more in the future.

If you've followed along with me so far, congratulations! By now, you should have an almost-finished website and a good many ideas about how to finish it. I suggest that you implement all of your ideas and finish building your website before going on to the next chapter, in which I'll show you how you can help search engines index your site better so that people can find it easily.

10

Optimizing for Search Engines

All right, you've built this terrific website. But what good is it if nobody can find it? Not much, you'll agree. So, the question that arises next is: how do you make your site "findable"?

And the answer is: by making your website friendlier to search engines.

The process of making your website friendlier to search engines is called **Search Engine Optimization***, or SEO in short.*

As it happens, there are more myths in the world of SEO than there are facts. In this chapter, I'll separate the wheat from the chaff. You'll learn:

- What SEO really is
- What it isn't
- What you can do to optimize your web pages for search engines

What is SEO?

Search engines use automated little programs, called bots or spiders, to scan the content of web pages and break it down into relevant words and phrases. Then, they add those words and phrases to an index. This process is called indexing. Bots routinely index millions of web pages and build massive indexes.

When a person uses a search engine to find a word or a phrase, the search engine looks up its index and generates a list of web pages on which the word or the phrase resides. The entries in this list are called search results. If the person searches for a word or a phrase, which is present on one of your web pages, it could appear in his search results.

However, the same words and phrases on your web pages are likely to be present on hundreds of thousands of pages on other websites as well. A search engine has to take an educated guess at which of those pages match the context of a user's query better than others and list them in the search results, in the order of their relevance. The position of your web page in relation to those of others among a set of search results is called your page's search engine position. Naturally, you'd want your web pages to be positioned among the first few results of a search. After all, nobody really has the patience to scroll down to entry number 21,497.

The problem, however, is that all those thousands of other pages are also vying for the same prime spots among the first few results of a user's query. So, how can you influence a search engine to list your web pages at the top of its search results at the expense of thousands of others?

A search engine determines the position of a web page in its results using a complex, and usually proprietary, formula called a search algorithm. The search algorithm is based on a diverse set of variables. Some of these variables are either published or easily guessed. Others are proprietary and esoteric. If you structure your web pages to conform to the way in which a search engine uses these variables, they are likely to achieve a better search engine position.

That, in essence, is the subject matter of SEO.

What SEO is not

With all this talk of influencing search engines, you might think that SEO is all about manipulating search engines into giving your web pages a bit more importance than they really deserve.

That's just not true!

You read that right. There's absolutely no sure-fire way of tricking search engines into favoring your web pages over those of others. Therefore, SEO is not some clever scheme to trick search engines or an insidious exploit of their deeply guarded secrets to your advantage. There are no magic tricks, no secrets, and no silver bullets.

There's no dearth of shady outfits which lead you into believing that they can do something special to make your site appear at the top of all search results in exchange for a small fortune, usually. In fact, there's a budding cottage industry built around SEO that's rivalled only by the mature cottage industry for preparing your kid to get into an Ivy League college. Unfortunately, they are both founded on myths, old wives' tales, and urban legends. And just for the record, getting your kid in to an Ivy League college might actually be easier.

Before you let a SEO service separate you from your money, consider this question: if every website-owner in your line of business pays a few bucks to monitor and improve his/her site's search-result positioning, whose site will actually show up at the top? You be the judge.

Optimizing your web pages

What exactly is SEO then? Simply put, SEO is the process of streamlining your web pages so that search engines can index them accurately and make informed decisions about their positioning. Optimizing your site is as easy as following a list of guidelines, a list of DOs and DON'Ts if you will, for building your web pages. When everybody follows these guidelines, search engines can do a better job of indexing web pages and presenting more meaningful results to users.

To that end, here's a list of specific DOs and DON'Ts:

Do comply with web standards

In a nutshell, web standards are sets of guidelines or specifications for developing web pages that will display correctly and provide all the intended functionality regardless of a user's location, hardware, operating system, browser, or disability.

Standards exist for almost every aspect of web development. HTML standards, for example, specify how to write correct HTML. Similarly, JavaScript standards specify how to write browser-independent scripts and accessibility guidelines specify how to make content available to people with varying preferences or physical abilities.

If you were to build a website without the help of Office Live Small Business's tools, you'd have to learn about all these standards. But because the tools do all of the heavy lifting for you, you don't have to. Now, that's both good and bad; good because you don't have to wrestle with all of those excruciating details and bad because you're forced to accept the markup that the tools generate, whether it complies with the standards or not.

You're not going to like what I'm about to say: the markup that Office Live Small Business generates for you isn't quite standards-compliant. But you can minimize the impact of non-standard markup if you use Office Live Small Business's tools wisely, as outlined in the guidelines below.

Do avoid HTML modules

The HTML module that you met in Chapter 9 is the main culprit that exacerbates non-standard markup on your web pages. True, you can customize the look and feel of your pages to your heart's content with HTML modules, but Office Live Small Business has to jump hoops to accommodate all of your customizations and make them compatible with the various browsers, computers, and operating systems out there. It also has to protect the content in your HTML modules to prevent the bad guys from defacing your site. The result is bloated, non-standard markup.

But don't panic! Just because you have a few HTML modules on your site doesn't mean that search engines will banish it to obscurity. So, don't get rid of them all. So long as you use them wisely, you'll do just fine. How do you use them wisely? Here are the simple rules:

- Do use them for showing external content such as clips hosted on MSN Video, product lists from Amazon Associates Program, or an Adobe Flash clip
- Don't use them for showing simple text; type it directly in a zone instead

The point is this: although I recommend avoiding HTML modules, there are situations where the only way to do what you wish to do is to use an HTML module, including a clip hosted on MSN Video, for example. When you find yourself in one of those situations, go ahead and use it. Remember, you shouldn't exclude relevant content from your site just because it would require you to use an HTML module.

 HTML modules have another flaw. Office Live Small Business loads their content dynamically using JavaScript. This means that a search engine's spiders can't see the content. That's another reason why you should avoid HTML modules. I built an entire site using HTML modules a couple of years ago only to find that it couldn't be indexed!

Do avoid Adobe Flash movies when HTML would do just fine

Search engines have a hard time indexing Adobe Flash content. Agreed, pages built with Flash are slicker than plain old HTML pages but they impede findability. It's okay to include a Flash movie on a page, but make sure that that's not the only content on the page. Supplement it with plain text in zones.

Do follow best practices

Once you've done all you can to comply with web standards, the next step is to follow a few basic conventions, or **best practices**, while building your web pages. Professional site developers often follow a long and stringent list of best practices. But because Office Live Small Business generates most of the markup on your website, your list is going to be rather small.

Specify a meaningful title for every page

By now, you're used to the drill—whenever you create a new web page, you provide a title for it. If you don't provide a title, Office Live Small Business puts one in for you. As it happens, the title plays a big role in how a search engine indexes a web page. So, you should make it a point to supply a meaningful title for every page that you create. I've insisted that you do so, but if you've ignored my advice, now's the time to make amends.

As you saw in Chapter 2, the title appears in a user's browser's title bar. My site's home page has the title **Home**, for example, and its contact page has the title **Contact the Author**, which appears in the browser like this:

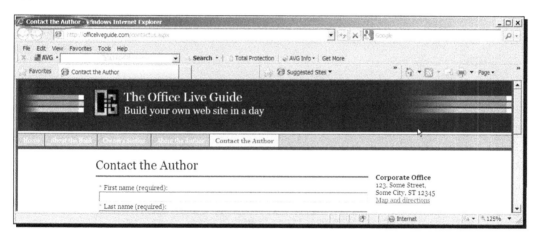

While this titles makes sense to a visitor in the context of my site, it doesn't do much to help a search engine categorize and index my site correctly. By convention, designers include the title of their websites in their page titles. The assumption is, that doing so helps search engines in indexing the site's web pages.

Some designers like to prefix the page title with the site title, others like to suffix it. The jury is still out on whether **The Office Live Guide—Contact the Author** or **Contact the Author—The Office Live Guide** is the better option. I suggest that you look at your favourite websites and decide which convention you'd like to follow.

Time for action – specifying meaningful page titles

1. Go to **Page Manager** and click on the **Properties** link for your site's **Contact Us** page. The **Choose page properties** dialog opens.

2. Change the **Page title** to include your site's title. For example, my page's title now reads: **The Office Live Guide – Contact the Author**, as shown in the next image:

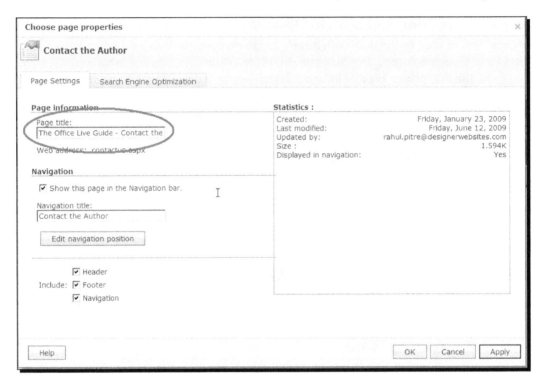

3. Click **OK**. The **Choose page properties** dialog closes.

4. Save your work and preview your site. Your **Contact Us** page should now be displaying your site's title as well. My page looks like this:

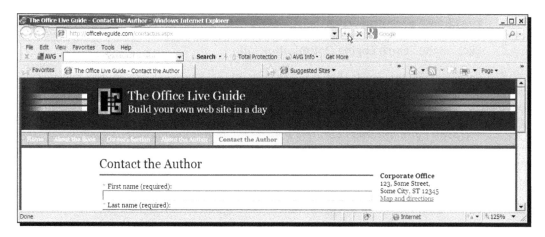

5. Now, follow this procedure for every page on your site.

What just happened?

You changed the title of one of your web pages to a more meaningful one. The change helps search engines index the page better. Although seemingly quite minor, this change alone impacts on the position of your web pages in search results more than anything else.

Specify keyword and description metatags wherever possible

Metatags are HTML tags that contain information about the page that contains them. The information resides on the page but it's not visible to a visitor viewing the page. Some metatags are a part of the official HTML specification but it's quite easy to create your own if that's what you want to do.

Each metatag has a name and also a value, which basically is the information that it contains. Metatags are used in web applications for a variety of purposes. Search engines use a couple of prominent metatags, the **Keyword** metatag and the **Description** metatag, for indexing pages appropriately.

The Keyword metatag tells a search engine which terms or keywords it should associate with your website. The Description metatag provides a brief description of what your site is about. If you provide pertinent information in these metatags, search engines can index your site more efficiently and, therefore, can include your site in the most relevant search results.

Time for action – specifying metatags

1. Go to **Page Manager** and click on the **Properties** link for your site's **Home** page. The **Choose page properties** dialog opens.

2. Click on the **Search Engine Optimization** tab.

3. Enter roughly ten words that come to your mind when you think of your business in the **Keyword metatags** box. (You can begin with the three words or phrases you wrote down in Pop Quiz 1.1 in Chapter 1.) Here's what I'll enter for my site:

   microsoft office live small business book rahul pitre small-business websites

   Notice that I haven't entered a sentence. I entered three phrases:

   microsoft office live small business book, **rahul pitre**, and **small-business websites**

   By doing so, I'm telling a search engine that if a person searches for any of these phrases, please include my site in the search results because that's what my site is about.

   Also, notice that all the words consist entirely of lower case letters; even my name. That's by convention.

Wouldn't my site appear in more search results if I included a thousand keywords?

That's what every logical person would think. Unfortunately, that's not the case. When you include a thousand keywords, you might end up confusing the search engine as to what exactly your site is about, and it may decide not to include your site in search results at all.

Nobody, except for the people who develop them, knows how search engines work. So, it's prudent to err on the side of caution and include few but precise keywords. That's the prevalent wisdom.

---

4. Enter a brief description of your site in roughly 30-50 words in the **Description metatag** box. Here's what I'll enter for my site:

   The Office Live Guide is a companion website to the book Microsoft Office Live Small Business: Beginner's Guide that teaches you how to build an attractive and effective website for your small business with Microsoft Office Live Small Business

   Again, notice that my description is brief. Keep yours brief too; don't write an essay. Remember that a computer program, and not a human, will be using it in its decision making process.

5. Your **Choose page properties** dialog should now look something like this:

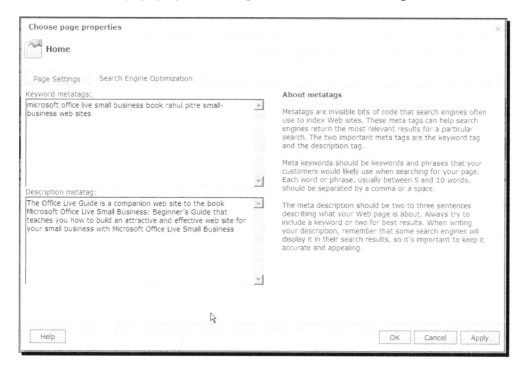

6. Click **OK**. The **Choose page properties** dialog closes.

7. Save your work.

What just happened?

You specified metatags for your site's **Home** page. As I mentioned before, the information in these tags doesn't actually show up on your website. So, if you preview your site, you won't notice any difference. But, hopefully, your efforts will pay off when your site appears in someone's search results.

Do you need these metatags on every page?

Not really. As a matter of fact, there's a trend of thought that modern search engines (read Google) don't use metatags at all any more. The trouble is that search engines don't confirm or deny the rumor. So, many designers like to include them on their web pages, just in case. Office Live Small Business has a provision for specifying both the metatags. Therefore, it's a good idea to add them to the most important pages on your site. I'd add them to the **Home** page and any product/service page on a website at the very least.

Fix broken links

A search engine's spiders traverse your site by following every link that they can find on your web pages. Therefore, it goes without saying that every link should lead to a valid web page. Broken links flummox the spiders and they may decide to abandon further traversal of your site.

There are several automated link validators for finding broken links. But their learning curve is somewhat steep for beginners. Because most small business websites are of manageable size, the easiest way of finding broken links is to click on every link on every page and make sure it goes to the page that it's supposed to go to. Many people find such manual checking too low-tech. They're not wrong but given the small size of your site, I heartily recommend it, especially, if you're a beginner.

By the way, you don't have to test navigation links on the primary and secondary navigation bars on your site; Office Live Small Business ensures that they're never broken. And you need to test links in your site's footer only from one page—any page you like. If they work from one page, they're guaranteed to work from all pages.

With the navigation and footer links out of the way, you should only have a handful of links to check manually.

Write good copy

Along with the page title and metatags, search engines use the text on your web pages to determine how to index them. Naturally, if they can make sense of the text on a page, they can index it correctly. You can help them make sense of the text by writing concise, to-the-point copy.

Check your spelling

When you take the trouble of writing good copy, it would be a shame if search engines can't make sense of your copy because you didn't spell-check the text. In this day and age, typos and spelling mistakes on web pages are unpardonable. So, CHECK YOUR SPELLING!

 Here's a word of caution: don't depend on your word processor's auto-correct or grammar-check options. Double-check your text manually.

Pop quiz 10.1

Are the following statements *true* or *false*?

1. It's a good idea to add many keyword metatags to your page. More metatags increase the chances of search engines including your page in more search results.

2. A meaningful page title plays a big role in determining the search engine positioning of your web pages.

3. SEO is all about tricking search engines into giving better positions to your web pages in their search results.

4. SEO services know secrets that can propel your web pages to the top of search engine results.

Don't abuse metatags

Use keyword metatags wisely. Add only a few relevant keywords to your pages, don't stuff them with hundreds of keyword metatags. Search engines can easily spot pages that have too many keywords and scant content. Moreover, don't add the same keyword metatag several times in an attempt to increase its importance. Although first-generation search engines were easily fooled by this trick, modern search engines have wisened-up to this shenanigan!

In the same vein, don't stuff the description metatag with every imaginable sentence that you think applies to your website. Just like fake keywords, search engines can identify fake descriptions too.

Don't add hidden text

A very common so-called trick is to add a lot of repetitive phrases to web pages as hidden text (or white text, as it is often called), that is, text that's displayed in the same font-color as the background color. Don't do it. Rest assured, you won't fool search engines with such simplistic tricks.

Don't link your pages to irrelevant pages

Don't pepper your web pages with spurious links to irrelevant destinations. You might have heard that search engines decide how popular your website is, based on the number of links on it. That's not true. They determine your site's popularity by looking at how many other websites link to yours; not how many you link yours to.

Don't fall prey to dubious SEO advice

This is the most important SEO advice that you can get: don't try to outsmart search engines. Dubious SEO advice abounds on the Web, a good bit of which is provided by people who don't quite understand how search engines work. As a rule of thumb, avoid anything that purports to outsmart search engines. Why? Because you just can't! The bright folks who build search engines are always a step ahead of the tricksters.

If search engines suspect you're cheating, they may "blacklist" your site and exclude it from their indexes altogether. Therefore, the best way to harness their power is to deal with them honestly. For your Office Live Small Business website, simply follow the advice in this chapter and leave the rest to the search engines.

Have a go hero – optimize your web pages

The set of SEO guidelines outlined in this chapter is, perhaps, the most important set of steps that you can take to optimize your web pages for search engines. Why not check how you've done so far in this department?

I recommend that you revisit each of your pages and check every little detail.

Summary

In this chapter, you learnt how to fine-tune your site so that search engines can index it efficiently and show it prominently in relevant searches. After working through it, you should find SEO to be less of a mystery. To recap:

- There's no magic trick to improving the position or rank of your website in search results; even if you're willing to pay!

- The best approach to SEO is to build web pages in such a way that helps search engines in classifying and indexing your pages appropriately so that they show up in the most relevant searches. You do so by conforming to standards, following best practices, and writing good content.

- Web standards are guidelines for building web pages the right way. You don't have much control over the standards your web pages follow because you don't write the HTML for your pages yourself; Office Live Small Business does this for you. Still, you can do something: avoid using HTML modules whenever possible because they don't produce standards-compliant markup.

- Although you don't have much control over standards compliance, you can certainly follow a few simple best practices to make your site friendlier to search engines.

- Specify meaningful page titles and metatags on your web pages, and write good meaningful copy. Above all, don't attempt to outsmart search engines. Follow these simple rules and you'll have done everything you can to make your site search engine-friendly.

That's all, folks! I hope you've enjoyed building your website along with me. Please check this book's companion website, www.officeliveguide.com, regularly for updates.

Signing Up: Opening a New Office Live Small Business Account

Signing up for Office Live Small Business is straightforward. You can breeze through it in ten minutes or less.

Finish in one sitting

Although the sign-up is quick, plan to finish up in a single sitting. If you stroll out for a cup of coffee halfway through it, this is what might greet you upon your return:

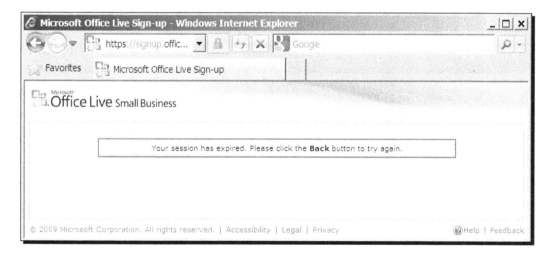

You'll then have to start the process all over again.

Signing up

To sign up for an account, follow these steps:

1. Point your browser at Office Live Small Business's home page, `www.officelive.com`. Here's what it looks like to someone in the United States at the time of writing this:

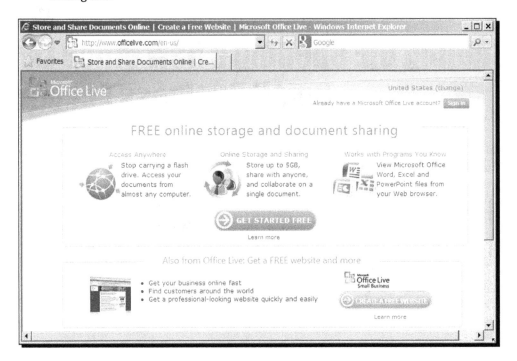

 Office Live Small Business is available in eight countries: Canada, France, Germany, India, Japan, Mexico, the United Kingdom, and the United States. The home page will take a guess at your country based on your IP address and display it above the green **Sign in** button in the top-right corner of the home page. If the guess is not on the money, click on the **(change)** link above the **Sign in** button. You'll arrive at the page that displays a list of countries where Office Live Small Business is available. Click on your country in the list and you'll arrive at the Office Live Small Business home page for your country.

2. Click on the **CREATE A FREE WEBSITE** button. The first page of the sign-up wizard appears as shown:

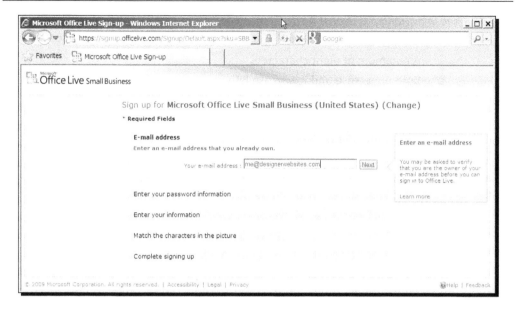

3. Enter your e-mail address. This e-mail address will be your login ID for your Office Live Small Business account. Click **Next**. Office Live Small Business asks you to enter the password you'll use for your account as shown:

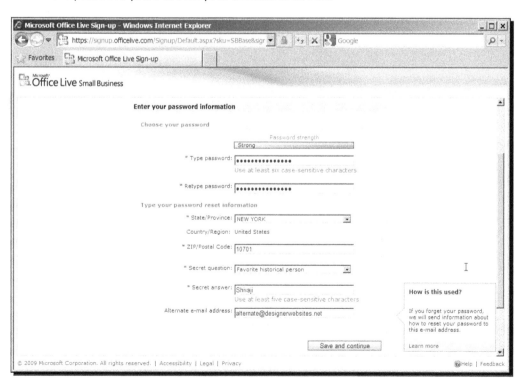

Choose a strong password! A strong password is one that's hard to guess and hard to crack with automated password-cracking tools. Your password should contain:

- A minimum of eight characters
- Both uppercase and lowercase letters
- At least one digit
- At least one special character, such as an underscore or the ampersand (&) symbol

The best way to come up with such a password is to choose the first character of each word in a phrase or a sentence because it's easy to remember. Think of a sentence, sometimes called a passphrase, such as We visited Labrador & Newfoundland in October 2009. Your password, then, could be WvL&NiO2.

By the way, don't use the name of a person or a place, personal information such as Social Security Number or date of birth, or a word in the dictionary as your password; hackers could guess or crack it easily.

And please, please, please don't use the word *password* itself as your password.

4. Enter your password and click **Save and continue**. Office Live Small Business asks you to enter some information about your business and yourself as shown:

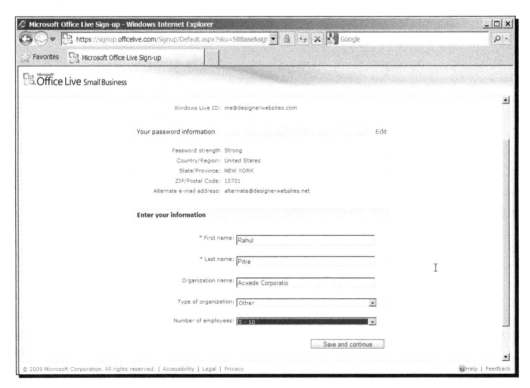

5. Complete the information requested and click **Save and continue**. Office Live Small Business displays a CAPTCHA to ensure that a human is filling out these forms as shown:

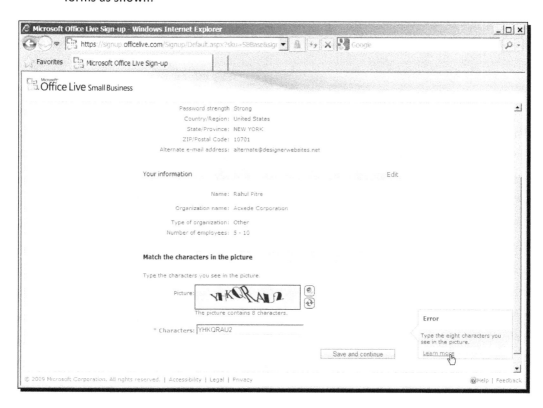

6. Enter the characters you see in the picture into the **Characters** textbox. Then, click **Save and continue**. Office Live Small Business asks you to accept the terms of service as shown:

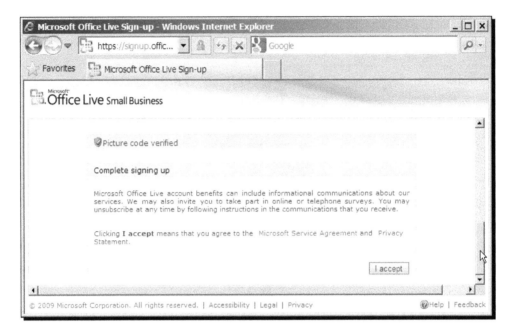

7. Read the **Microsoft Service Agreement** and the **Privacy Statement**. If you agree to both, click **I accept**.

Congratulations! You are now a proud owner of a spanking new Office Live Small Business account.

B

Setting Up E-mail Accounts

As you'd expect, Office Live Small Business provides you with e-mail accounts for your domain. Let me show you how to create and manage them.

Creating an e-mail account

To create an e-mail account, follow these steps:

1. Sign in to your Office Live Small Business account.

2. Pull down the **More** menu from the top navigation bar and then choose **Account Management**. The **Account Management** page appears.

3. Click **E-mail Accounts** in the left navigation pane. The **E-mail Accounts** page appears as shown:

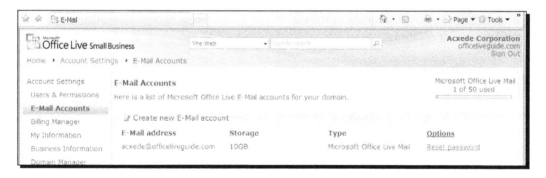

4. Click on the **Create new E-Mail account** icon on the actions bar. The **Create new E-Mail account** dialog appears. Type all the information requested. Note that you can only type the portion of the e-mail address before the @ symbol. Office Live Small Business sets the domain name automatically as shown:

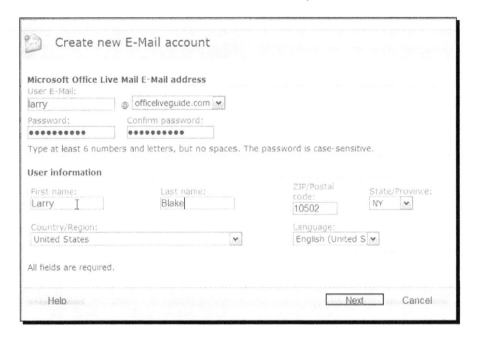

5. Click **Next**. After a brief delay, the **Summary dialog** informs you that the account has been created.

6. Click **Finish**. You'll return to the **E-mail** page, which now lists the e-mail address that you just created.

Resetting the password of an e-mail account

You may want to reset the password for an e-mail account in two situations:

◆ If a user forgets his password and asks you for help

◆ If you want to prevent the owner of an account from accessing his e-mail for some reason; for example, he stopped working for you

To reset the password for an e-mail account, follow these steps:

1. Sign in to your Office Live Small Business account.

2. Pull down the **More** menu from the top navigation bar and then choose **Account Management**. The **Account Management** page appears.

3. Click **E-mail Accounts** in the left navigation pane. The **E-mail Accounts** page appears. It displays a list of all of the e-mail accounts in your domain.

4. Click the **Reset password** link in the **Options** column of the e-mail account for which you want to reset the password. The **Reset account password** dialog appears. Enter a new password, and then retype it in the **Confirm password** box as shown:

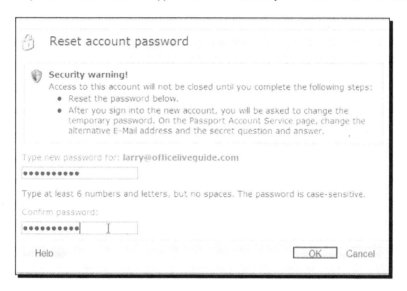

5. Click **OK**. You should see the **Account password reset confirmation** dialog confirming the change as shown:

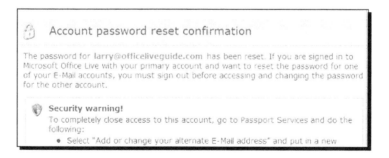

Although you see a **Security warning** in the **Reset account password** dialog, you haven't done anything wrong. The dialog draws your attention to the fact that although you've changed the password on the e-mail account, the owner of the account can still use other identifying information on the account, such as the secret question and the alternate e-mail address, to retrieve the password.

You don't have to worry about this if you've changed the password simply because the account owner forgot it. But if you changed it because you wish to prevent the account owner from accessing mail at this address, you must change the identifying information as well.

The Windows Live ID authentication system (called Passport Account Services in its previous incarnation) maintains the identifying information. To change it:

❑ Click the **Go to Passport Account Services** link at the bottom of the **Account password reset confirmation** dialog.

❑ Log in to the e-mail account with the new password that you just created, and change the identifying information.

Deleting an e-mail account

You may delete any e-mail account from your domain. To delete one, follow these steps:

1. Sign in to your Office Live Small Business Account.

2. Pull down the **More** menu from the top navigation bar and then choose **Account Management**. The **Account Management** page appears.

3. Click **E-mail Accounts** in the left navigation pane. The **E-mail Accounts** page appears. It displays a list of all the e-mail accounts in your domain.

4. Click the **Delete** link in the **Options** column of the e-mail account you want to delete. The **Delete account** dialog appears as shown:

5. Read the warning very carefully. If you're sure that you want to delete the account, click **Delete**.

Warning

Once you delete an e-mail account, you can't create it again for 130 days!

6. The **Account deleted** dialog appears to inform you that the e-mail account has been deleted as shown:

 Account deleted

The following E-Mail address has been deleted:

larry@officeliveguide.com

7. Click **Close**.

Change password

Change passwords of e-mail accounts instead of deleting them.

 When you delete an e-mail account, all the mail in the associated mailbox is deleted as well. If all you want to do is to stop the owner of an e-mail account from accessing it, reset its password and identifying information.

Let's say your Marketing Manager resigns. You'll naturally want to prevent him from accessing his mailbox any longer. But deleting his e-mail account will get rid of all the mail in his mailbox as well. When you change the password on the e-mail account, you will still be able to read and send mail from it, but your ex-Marketing Manager won't be able to access it any longer.

C

Submitting Your Site to Search Engines

If you've earnestly followed the SEO guidelines in the book (Chapter 10 in particular), your site is already optimized for search engines. All you need to do now is to submit it to the top three search engines by visiting their respective submission pages:

- **Google:** `www.google.com/addurl/?continue=/addurl`
- **Yahoo!:** `http://search.yahoo.com/info/submit.html`
- **Bing:** `http://www.bing.com/docs/submit.aspx`

It takes a few days for the search engines to index your site, but there are no guarantees as to when it will start showing up in their search results. Of two sites submitted simultaneously, one may get indexed overnight, and the other may languish mysteriously for a couple of months.

Typically, your site will appear fairly quickly in Bing's and Yahoo!'s search results. It often takes agonizingly long, however, to appear in Google's.

To check whether the search engines have indexed your site, you can query them like this:

- **Google:** Type *site:yourdomain.com* in Google's search box at `http://www.google.com` and press *Enter*. If your site is indexed, you'll see one or more of your web pages in the results. If not, you'll see a message that says: **Your search -** *site: yourdomain.com* **- did not match any documents**.
- **Yahoo!:** Go to `http://search.yahoo.com/search/options`. The page has several search options. The one you need is **Site/Domain**. Choose the last radio button, next to the option that says **only search in this domain/site:**. Then, type the name of your domain (*yourdomain.com*), in the textbox next to it and press *Enter*. If your site has already been indexed, you'll see a link to your home page in the results. If not, you'll see a message that says: **We were unable to find any results for the given URL in our index:** *http://yourdomain.com*.

- **Bing:** Type your domain name, *yourdomain.com*, in the Bing search box at `http://www.bing.com` and press *Enter*. If your site has been indexed, a link to your home page will appear in the results. If not, you'll see a message that says: **We did not find any results for** *yourdomain.com*.

 In the discussion above, *yourdomain.com* is the name of your domain. To check on my website, I'll have to type **officeliveguide.com**. Note that there's no *http://* or *www.* in the domain name.

You may have heard that there are hundreds of search engines and that there are paid search engine services that submit your site to many of them. So, why am I content in advising you to submit your site to only the top three? Because over 99% of the Web's search engine traffic flows through the big three; the rest of them aren't going to buy you much.

Finally, I'll reiterate the advice that I offered in Chapter 10: don't try to manipulate search engines using paid search services. If you've done your job of building a search engine-friendly website, the search engines will do theirs automatically.

D

Backup and Restore: Recovering From Disasters

There are many ways of losing files that you've stored on a computer. The hard disk that stores the file could crash, for example, or some inexplicable event could corrupt it to the point of being unusable. You might even push the wrong button accidentally and end up saying sayonara to an important file.

Because your web pages, and pictures on them, are ultimately stored as files, they too are prone to such mishaps. The only way to safeguard your files is to back them up periodically.

Office Live Small Business lets you make back up copies of everything on your website and provides facilities to restore it from the back a copy, if need be.

Backing Up

To back up your website, follow these steps:

1. Sign in to your Office Live Small Business account, if you haven't done so already, and go to **Page Manager**.

2. Click on the **Site actions** tile to pull down the **Site actions** menu and then choose **Back up or restore** as shown in the following screenshot:

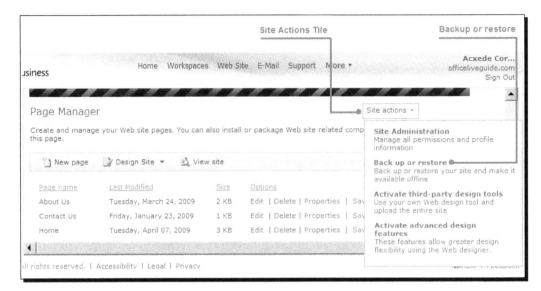

3. The **Back up or restore Website** page appears as shown:

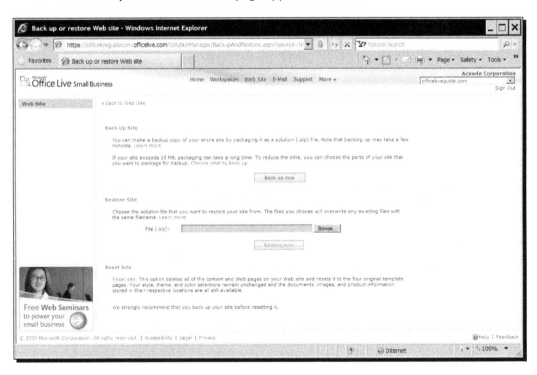

4. The page has three sections: **Back Up Site**, **Restore Site**, and **Reset Site**. Each of them helps you to do exactly what it says.

Caution

Be very careful with the **Reset Site** option. As its on-screen description informs you, it wipes your site clean and replaces it with the starter website that you first saw in Chapter 1.

5. You have an option of backing up either a few selected pages or the entire website. If you wish to back up only a few files, you can select those files by clicking on the **Choose what to back up** link. But, I recommend backing up the entire website. To that end, click the **Back up now** button. Office Live Small Business tells you that it's working on your request as shown:

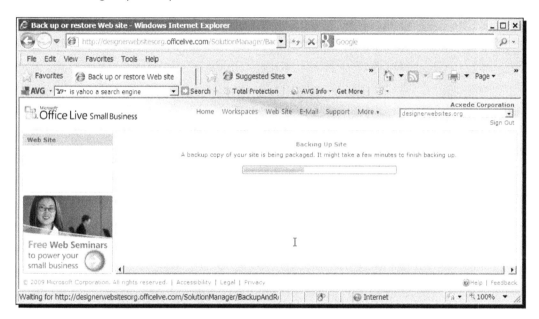

Site Backup

All too frequently, Office Live Small Business will tell you that it couldn't back your site up:

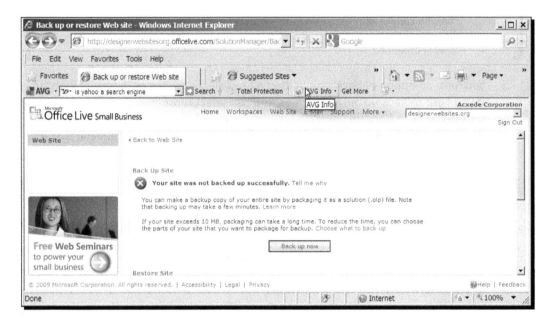

That's usually because the servers are busy. Try again after some time and the process should succeed.

6. Office Live Small Business saves the backup in a file with a `.olp` extension. When the back up is done, you'll see a prompt to save the `.olp` file.

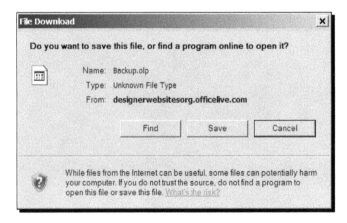

7. Save the file to a location on your computer.

 Office Live Small Business saves the backed up files in a proprietary format; you can't see or access individual files in a `.olp` file.

Restoring

To restore your site, follow these steps:

1. Before you restore your site from a backup, it's a good idea to make another backup of it in its present state. Otherwise, if the restore operation fails, for whatever reason, you'll be left with no website at all!

2. To restore your site from a backup, go to **Page Manager** and click on the **Site actions** tile to pull down the **Site actions** menu and then choose **Backup or restore**.

3. The **Back up or restore Web site** page appears as shown:

4. Click the **Browse** button under **Restore site** and choose the `.olp` file that contains the backup you want to restore from.

5. Click **Restore now**. Office Live Small Business informs you that it will wipe parts of your site clean while restoring it and will remind you to take another backup in its present state. As you've already done so in step 1, click **OK**.

6. After a brief pause, Office Live Small Business informs you that the restore was successful as shown:

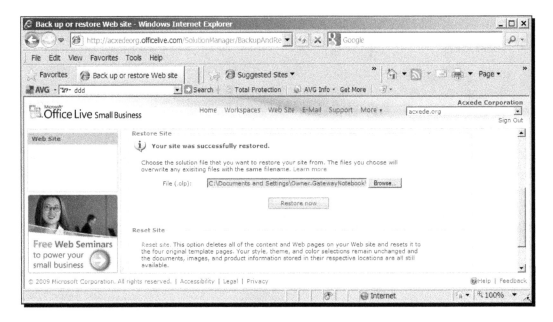

Reports: Analyzing Visitor Statistics

Okay, you've built a terrific website. You're convinced that it's attractive, informative, and user-friendly. The question, however, is whether other people think so too.

And how do find that out? Elementary, my dear Watson! All you need to do is snoop around for information such as the following:

- How many people visited your website in a given period?

- Which search engines or directories did they use to arrive there?

- Which keywords did they type into search engines to find your website?

- How long did people stay on your website once they got there?

- Which pages did they visit the most?

- Which pages appeared to drive visitors away?

- What kind of computers and browsers did your visitors use?

- Did your online advertising campaigns generate enough traffic to justify the expense?

Once you find answers to these questions, you can put two and two together and take an educated guess at the ultimate question: *Does my website fulfill its objectives?*

To help you find answers to these questions easily, Office Live Small Business automatically embeds a little chunk of JavaScript on each of your web pages. The script sends back the dirt on every page request that your website gets, such as the IP address of the visitor's computer, the name of the page that they requested, and the brand and version of their browser. Office Live Small Business stores all of these details in a database.

A set of reports, called **Reports**, then extracts this information from the database on Office Live Small Business's servers on demand, compiles it logically, and presents it as easy-to-understand charts and tables that you can make sense of easily.

Tools, such as Reports, which gather and analyze a website's visitor statistics are called *web analytics packages*. The most well-known web analytics package, perhaps, is Google Analytics.

Accessing Reports

To access **Reports**, sign in to your Office Live Small Business account, if you haven't done so already, and go to **Page Manager**. Click on the **Reports** link in the left navigation bar. The **Reports** dashboard page appears. It displays a few metrics graphically. You'll see several links in the left navigation bar of the dashboard. Each of them will lead you to a report.

What exactly do these Reports tell you?

A website's visitor statistics is not a single, monolithic number; several related attributes make up these statistics. To make sense of the numbers as you view the various reports, you must know what those attributes are and what they mean. So, here's the vernacular:

 Keep in mind that these definitions are specific to **Reports**; other web analytics packages may have different meanings for these terms.

- ◆ **Visitors**: A *visitor* is a person who requests a page from a website.

- ◆ **Page views**: A *page view* represents a visitor accessing a page on a website.

- ◆ **Visits**: Everything that a visitor does on a website before leaving it constitutes a *visit*. A visit results in one or more page views. If a visitor doesn't do anything for a while, usually 30 minutes, the visit ends.

- ◆ **New and returning visitors**: A person paying his first visit to a website is a *new visitor*. His second visit onward, he becomes a *returning visitor*. Websites distinguish between new and returning visitors based on their IP addresses, by giving them cookies, or some combination thereof. Let's say the same person arrives at a website at two different times. If you view Reports between his first and second visits, it will show one visit and one new visitor. If you view Reports after the second visit, it will show two visits and one returning visitor.

- ◆ **Unique visitors**: The term *unique visitors* refers to the number of distinct people who visit a website. If a person visits a website three times, the web server records three visits, but only one unique visitor. From the Report's point of view:

  Unique Visitors = New Visitors + Returning Visitors

◆ **Entry pages**: An *entry page* is the first page on a website that a visitor views during a given visit. Say a website has three pages: Home, Products, and Contact Us. If a visitor clicks on a link in the search-engine results that brings him to the Products page, then it is the entry page for that visit.

◆ **Exit pages**: An *exit page* is the last page on a website that a visitor views during a given visit. Continuing with the example in the previous entry, if the visitor views the Contact Us page after entering the site at the Products page and then surfs away to another site, the Contact Us page is the exit page for that visit.

◆ **Sources**: A visitor arrives at a website either by clicking on a link on another website or by typing the website's address in his browser's address bar. If he arrives from another website, that website is the *source* or the *referrer* for his visit. If, on the other hand, he types the website's address in his browser's address bar, a direct link is the source for his visit.

◆ **Referrer pages**: The specific page, on the source website, on which a visitor clicks a link to arrive at a website, is the *referrer page*. A referrer page is of interest only if it's not a search results page of a search engine. If it is, the keyword(s) that the visitor entered for the search are more relevant.

◆ **Keywords**: *Keywords* are the words, terms, or phrases that people search for using search engines. If you search for the words *Office Live*, those are the keywords.

◆ **Conversions and Conversion points**: The main reason that people build websites is to lure visitors into taking an action, whether that's to buy an item, ask for a quote, or give feedback. When a visitor takes such a desired action, he makes a *conversion* and reaches a *conversion point*. Let's say a website's primary purpose is to sell some items and to that end, the website has a shopping cart. Let's also assume that after a visitor places an order by checking out from the shopping cart, the website displays an order confirmation page. Now, everytime someone reaches the order confirmation page, he takes an action that the site's owners want him to take. Therefore, he makes a conversion and the order confirmation page is conversion point.

◆ **Conversion rate**: The *conversion rate* tells you how often visitors to a website reach a conversion point. If five out of every hundred visits result in a conversion, the conversion rate is 5%.

What Reports don't tell you

Let me squash a myth before we go any further: contrary to common belief, Reports, or any other web analytics package for that matter, doesn't offer a prescription to propel your website to the very top of all search results, nor does it prescribe the magic pill that would compel people all over the world to ditch their favorite websites and flock to yours.

I'm sure you'd be overjoyed to receive a bulleted list from Reports every morning that goes something like this:

◆ Add five more pages to your site with such-and-such content; that's what people are looking for.

◆ Change the background color of your web pages to light blue and change the font from Verdana to Georgia. That should attract 63 additional visitors every day!

◆ The third word on the 24th line of the Services page is spelt *promtp*. It should be prompt. By the way, the copy on the Services page is just pitiful. Replace it with this: [new copy here]. Not only will this increase traffic by 11%, your visitors will start clicking on the AdSense ads on the web page as well.

Unfortunately, Reports can't generate such a list. They merely present site statistics in an easy-to-understand format. What you do with those numbers is entirely up to you.

The right way to use Reports

Details of a single visit can't give you a peek into your visitors' minds, but when you consolidate details from hundreds or thousands of visits, you begin to notice trends in their behavior. These trends tell you whether your web site's visitors are using your website the way that you want them to. If they aren't, corrective measures are in order.

Trends are difficult to identify from only the raw data. They're far easier to notice when you review scientifically grouped data over a long period of time. Therefore, interpreting Reports is not a one-time activity; it's an ongoing 3-step process:

1. Review reports periodically. For small websites, once a month is usually enough.

2. Analyze the trends and individual metrics in them to see if anything appears amiss and take an educated guess as to why. Are fewer people visiting your site over a period of time? Are they visiting only a page or two instead of browsing around the entire site? Does a specific page appear frequently among exit pages, and if so, could it be so because the page is not displaying (or working) correctly? These are the kind of questions that you should be looking to answer with Reports.

3. Make changes to your website to address the likely problem areas and go back to step 1 to evaluate how effective your changes were (and to find new problem areas).

The second step is the key step in this process. If you're able to pinpoint the problem areas effectively, you'll have a better shot at attaining the goals that you've set for your website.

The wrong way to use Reports

As a new site owner, you might be tempted to pore over your site statistics several times a day and tweak a few things on your website here and there. Rest assured, it won't serve any purpose; heck, it may even lead you to the wrong conclusions.

It's very easy to twist statistics and draw nonsensical conclusions from them. There's the story of a man, for example, who was found dead with his head in the oven and his feet in the refrigerator. The coroner put down *exposure to extreme temperatures* as the cause of death. The statisticians were puzzled, however, because according to their calculations, he was at room temperature, on average, at the time of his death.

To avoid such traps, keep in mind that:

- ◆ Statistics are relevant only when there's enough data. If you look at the statistics of a popular website that several thousand people visit every day, you may be able to notice trends every day or even every hour, perhaps. But that may not be true of a small website, such as yours, which far fewer people visit every day. Therefore, you might have to wait a long time before you have enough data to make sense of the numbers.

- ◆ Raw numbers tell you very little. Let's say, for example, that 956 people visited my website yesterday and they viewed 4539 pages. Is that good or bad? You can't really tell because you don't have a meaningful frame of reference. But if I tell you that 352 people viewed 1127 pages the day before, you can then put yesterday's numbers in perspective.

Are Reports accurate?

Gathering visitor statistics isn't an exact science. Like all statistics, visitor statistics too have an inherent margin of error. The numbers can get distorted, as the following examples illustrate:

- ◆ If two people who visit a website are behind the same proxy server, the web server may not recognize them as distinct visitors because both expose the same IP address to the web server.

- ◆ If a single person uses an Internet service that doesn't necessarily route separate page requests to the same website through the same proxy server—AOL, for example, the web server may record each page request as coming from a distinct visitor.

- ◆ The term *visit* doesn't have a universally-accepted definition. What constitutes a single visit to a person may appear to be two different visits to a web server. For example, you may get a call from a friend soon after you visit a website. You may chat with your friend for an hour and then go back to your computer and continue from where you left off. From your perspective, you visited the website only once. The site's web server, however, may have stopped keeping track of you after, say, 30 minutes. When you resume your interrupted visit, the server then may record it as a distinct visit.

- ◆ Sometimes, web servers record visitors based on a unique cookie that they issue to each visitor. This approach has two advantages: visits by robots are ignored because they don't accept cookies, and multiple visits by the same person can be tracked to get a more accurate count of unique visitors. But this system is not foolproof either. If you visit a site from your work computer as well as from your home computer, the web server may count you as two distinct visitors.

Such distortions tend to even out as the volume of the data increases. It's difficult or even pointless to analyze data that consists of all of five visits, but as the volume grows, you can consider Reports accurate enough for all practical purposes.

What about Google Analytics?

Google Analytics is perhaps the best hosted web analytics tool. It has a comprehensive feature-set. Its slick, interactive reports illuminate every imaginable web-traffic statistic. And to top it all, it has an unbeatable price tag: free!

The main reason for its universal adoption, however, is that it's integrated with AdWords, Google's advertisement-placement service. If you advertise with AdWords, you can easily track the effectiveness of each ad campaign with Google Analytics. For anyone who spends advertising dollars on AdWords, Google Analytics is an indispensable tool.

But Google Analytics has a lot to offer even if you don't use AdWords. The statistical reports it produces are comprehensive. They help you to tailor your site's content to a visitor's requirements.

Besides, you can customize Google Analytics' reports to suit your specific requirements. Here's an example: if you monitor web statistics faithfully, it makes sense to filter out visits from you and your employees. The Reports package doesn't have settings to filter out such internal traffic. If you expect your website to have a significant amount of internally generated traffic, you may be at a serious disadvantage using Reports.

Google Analytics' reports are state-of-the-art. Many web analytics pros consider entry pages and exit pages to be 'so 20th century'. Reports, unfortunately, don't support newer metrics like click density, which identifies the hot spots on your web pages where visitors tend to click the most.

Despite all its limitations, however, don't dismiss Reports summarily. Remember the following:

- Reports suffice for the needs of small websites and novice webmasters. If you're just starting out with web analytics, Google Analytics can be somewhat overwhelming.

- Like Google Analytics, Reports are free too. And if you use adManager, Microsoft's AdWords-like service, you're better off with Site Reports, which have built-in support for tracking adManager campaigns.

- Reports are integrated with Office Live Small Business, which automatically adds the little chunk of JavaScript tracking code. Therefore, you don't have to open yet another account with Google Analytics and add its JavaScript code manually to your web pages.

- You must be familiar with HTML and JavaScript in order to integrate Google Analytics with your Office Live Small Business website. The straightforward instructions on Google Analytics' website won't work with Office Live Small Business because of the way that **Page Editor** builds web pages.

My advice, therefore, is to start off with Reports if you're new to web analytics. Use the package for a while and get a feel for web analytics. After using Reports for a few months, if you feel that the package's simplicity is holding you back, by all means switch to Google Analytics.

F
Answers to Pop Quizes

Answers to Pop quiz 1.1

1. Click the **Edit** link against the **Home** page in **Page Manager**'s page list.

2. Pull down the **Web pages** menu in **Page Editor**'s top left-hand corner. It lists all the pages on your website.

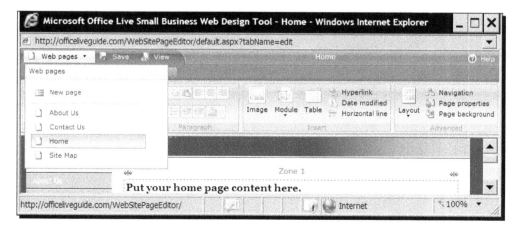

The current page in **Page Editor,** in this case, **Home,** is highlighted. Click **About Us** in the pull-down menu to bring that page up in **Page Editor**.

Answer to Pop quiz 2.1

1. Which of the following attributes make your website more "findable"?

    B—your site's title and D—your site's slogan. These elements help search engines index your site correctly. Therefore, it's more likely to show up in relevant search results.

Answer to Pop quiz 3.1

1. **Georgia** and **Verdana** are the preferred fonts for websites because:

    B. They were designed especially for monitors. Therefore, they're easier to read on-screen.

Answer to Pop quiz 4.1

1. *Your website's* **Advanced design Features** enable *you to:*

    B. Tweak design features not exposed in the **Site Designer** or the **Page Editor**. You can create page templates, for example, and customize the width of your site beyond the options available in the **Site Designer**.

Answer to Pop quiz 6.1

1. How many levels of navigation can a website built with Office Live Small Business have?

    B. A website built with Office Live Small Business can have two levels of navigation at the most.

Answers to Pop quiz 7.1

1. In Office Live Small Business's lingo, a Module is:

    B. A pre-packged mini-program that you can drop on a web page and configure it to perform a predetermined task

2. Although it is possible to optimize pictures in Image Uploader, it's not a very good idea because optimized pictures make web pages sluggish. True or false?

    False. Optimization reduces a picture's file size. Pages with smaller pictures load faster.

3. Downloading pictures from other people's websites and using them on yours amounts to stealing. Therefore you should hyperlink to those pictures instead. Right or wrong?

    Wrong. When you link to pictures on other websites, you're stealing bandwidth in effect.

Answer to Pop quiz 8.1

1. Which of the following is NOT valid hexadecimal color code?

    C. Hexadecimal codes can only contain the numbers 0-9 and the letters a through f. They are not case sensitive. Therefore, A, B, and D are valid codes.

Answers to Pop quiz 9.1

1. HTML contains instructions on

    A. Formatting the text and other content on a web page

2. You found this HTML markup on a web page:

    `<strong>elephant</strong>`

    What do you think the markup does?

    B. It displays the word elephant in bold letters when the web page is displayed in a browser

Answers to Pop quiz 10.1

True or false?

1. It's a good idea to add many keyword metatags to your page. More metatags increase the chances of search engines including your page in more search results.

   False.

2. A meaningful page title plays a big role in determining the search engine positioning of your web pages.

   True.

3. SEO is all about tricking search engines in to giving better positions to your web pages in their search results.

   False.

4. SEO services know secrets that can propel your web pages to the top of search engine results.

   False.

Index

Thank you for buying
Microsoft Office Live Small Business

About Packt Publishing

Packt, pronounced 'packed', published its first book "*Mastering phpMyAdmin for Effective MySQL Management*" in April 2004 and subsequently continued to specialize in publishing highly focused books on specific technologies and solutions.

Our books and publications share the experiences of your fellow IT professionals in adapting and customizing today's systems, applications, and frameworks. Our solution based books give you the knowledge and power to customize the software and technologies you're using to get the job done. Packt books are more specific and less general than the IT books you have seen in the past. Our unique business model allows us to bring you more focused information, giving you more of what you need to know, and less of what you don't.

Packt is a modern, yet unique publishing company, which focuses on producing quality, cutting-edge books for communities of developers, administrators, and newbies alike. For more information, please visit our website: www.packtpub.com.

Writing for Packt

We welcome all inquiries from people who are interested in authoring. Book proposals should be sent to author@packtpub.com. If your book idea is still at an early stage and you would like to discuss it first before writing a formal book proposal, contact us; one of our commissioning editors will get in touch with you.

We're not just looking for published authors; if you have strong technical skills but no writing experience, our experienced editors can help you develop a writing career, or simply get some additional reward for your expertise.

PUBLISHING

WordPress for Business Bloggers

ISBN: 978-1-847195-32-6   Paperback: 356 pages

Promote and grow your WordPress blog with advanced plug-ins, analytics, advertising, and SEO

1. Gain a competitive advantage with a well polished WordPress business blog

2. Develop and transform your blog with strategic goals

3. Create your own custom design using the Sandbox theme

4. Apply SEO (search engine optimization) to your blog

5. Market and measure the success of your blog

SharePoint Designer Tutorial

ISBN: 978-1-847194-42-8   Paperback: 170 pages

Get started with SharePoint Designer and learn to put together a business website with SharePoint

1. Become comfortable in the SharePoint Designer environment

2. Learn about SharePoint Designer features as you create a SharePoint website

3. Step-by-step instructions and careful explanations

Please check **www.PacktPub.com** for information on our titles

WordPress 2.7 Cookbook

ISBN: 978-1-847197-38-2   Paperback: 316 pages

100 simple but incredibly useful recipes to take control of your WordPress blog layout, themes, widgets, plug-ins, security, and SEO

1. Take your WordPress blog to the next level with solutions to common WordPress problems that make your blog better, smarter, faster, and more secure

2. Enhance your SEO and make more money online by applying simple hacks

3. Fully tested and compatible with WordPress 2.7

4. Part of Packt's Cookbook series: Each recipe is a carefully organized sequence of instructions to complete the task as efficiently as possible

Small Business Server 2008

ISBN: 978-1-847196-30-9   Paperback: 408 pages

Set up and run your small business server making it deliver big business impact

1. Step-by-step guidance through the installation and configuration process with numerous pictures

2. Successfully install SBS 2008 into your business, either as a new installation or by migrating from SBS 2003

3. Configure hosted web sites for public and secure information exchange using Office Live for Small Business and Office Live Workspaces

Please check **www.PacktPub.com** for information on our titles

www.ingramcontent.com/pod-product-compliance
Lightning Source LLC
Chambersburg PA
CBHW060539060326
40690CB00017B/3539